Tilting your teaching

7 simple shifts that can substantially improve student learning

McREL
INTERNATIONAL
Denver, Colorado USA

Glen Pearsall
with **Natasha Harris**

McREL International
4601 DTC Boulevard, Suite 500
Denver, CO 80237 USA
Phone: 303.337.0990 | Fax: 303.337.3005
Website: www.mcrel.org | Email: info@mcrel.org | Store: store.mcrel.org

Copyright © 2020 by McREL International. All rights reserved. This book and its contents are intended for individual use by the purchaser. You may make copies of the tools for personal classroom use only. Except for that usage, no part of this publication may be reproduced or transmitted in any form or by any means without the prior written permission of the publisher.

_____

About McREL

McREL International is a nonprofit education research and development organization that turns knowledge about what works in education into practical, effective resources and services to help teachers and education leaders flourish.

_____

All referenced trademarks are the property of the respective owners. All internet links mentioned in this book are correct as of the initial publication date.

Printed in the United States of America.

To order, visit store.mcrel.org.

Cover artwork by Geronimo Creative Services.

ISBN: 978-1-7347820-0-4

Library of Congress Control Number: 2020905198

Pearsall, G., & Harris, N. (2020). *Tilting your teaching: Seven simple shifts that can substantially improve student learning.* McREL International.

Tilting your teaching

7 simple shifts that can substantially improve student learning

Dedication and Acknowledgments ii
Introduction iii
Simple Shifts 1
Shift One: Low-Key Interventions 11
Shift Two: Pivoting and Reframing 25
Shift Three: Instructional Clarity 45
Shift Four: Wait Time 63
Shift Five: Pause and Elaboration Time 77
Shift Six: Snapshot Feedback 91
Shift Seven: Reflection Time 109
Conclusion: A New Way of Looking at Teaching 129
References 133
About the Authors 138
Reproducibles 139

To Noah & Jem: The Unstoppable Force and the Immovable Object.

Thanks to Bryan Goodwin, Ron Miletta, and the team at McREL. Thanks also to all the teachers who have been brave enough to share their teaching in video coaching sessions—we may have changed some details to protect your privacy, but you will recognize your hard work, dedication, and expertise in the pages of this book.

Introduction

The first time I saw a Fitbit it was worn by a PE teacher I was coaching. We'd finished our coaching session at the junior campus of his school and, as both of us were working at the senior campus that afternoon, I offered to drive him. He said he would walk. This surprised me: It was a long walk back to the senior campus and he'd just finished telling me of a 20 km run he'd done before work.

"Didn't you train already this morning?" I asked.

"Yes, but I want to get my steps up," he said, pointing to his Fitbit.

"Steps up?"

"Yes, it records my steps and when I get to 10,000 there's a reward."

"What's the reward?"

He looked at me, wide-eyed and earnest: "It buzzes."

The contrast between his enthusiasm and the reward struck me—it was a small payoff for all that effort. However, instant feedback can be compelling like that. Quick feedback loops are a powerful motivator.

The more I thought about it, the more I appreciated how this loop was designed. I particularly appreciated the insight of concentrating on *steps*—it seemed such a clever way to get people more active. There are lots of other potential metrics you could use to encourage a less sedentary lifestyle—total times exercised in a week, average km run a day—but 10,000 steps seemed such a deft little nudge; a simple shift of everyday routine that could lead to a cascade of other little lifestyle changes and benefits. It made me wonder . . .

What would the equivalent of focusing on *steps* be for teachers? What little changes of technique would lead quickly to a host of other improvements?

And what would a Fitbit for teachers look like? Are there tools for prompting these changes and measuring their impact?

In this book, I want to explore seven examples of these small but powerful changes of practice—the "Simple Shifts." In the chapter titled Simple Shifts, I'll introduce the Simple Shifts for teachers, and explain why each of these is a skill that will lead to larger change for your students and yourself. Then we'll explore in more detail the mechanics of changing practice, and what the latest research can tell us about *how* to change our teaching practice. I'll introduce you to "micro-data tools": one of the most effective ways I have found to consolidate a new skill and embed it within your routine teaching practice.

The subsequent chapters will all follow a similar structure: We'll look at one Simple Shift in detail; explore variations of the basic skill, troubleshooting options, and inflection points; and I'll detail the micro-data tools most effective for tracking your development of this Simple Shift.

As teachers, we already work hard enough. We need more than just another set of great teaching techniques to learn—there are so many strategies you might adopt to improve your practice and often very little available time to identify which will make the biggest impact. What we need are compelling reasons to choose one skill over another, and a clear plan of *how* we are going to implement these skills that is simple enough to start with the very next lesson.

Developed from extensive research and decades of teaching experience, the Simple Shifts meet this goal. They do not require you to totally change your teaching but to "tilt" it. Quick to learn and easy to implement, they are minor adjustments of your practice that nonetheless can have a major impact on your students' learning.

Simple Shifts

As a teacher, I encountered lots of able learners but I also came across *efficient* learners—students who were able to identify the core learning in a task and concentrate their efforts on that aspect of what we were doing. Often, these were students who took real pleasure in their strategic insight.

I taught one Year 12 student who had transferred in and missed the first two weeks of my classes, but came in, mastered a key essay-writing technique in an after-school session, and then produced an outstanding essay for the assessment task on the entire unit. "It was easy," he told his classmates. "I'd already read the book so I just had to find out what the main trick behind this kind of essay writing is and do that." (The student sitting next to him looked disappointed: "So you still had to read the book?")

Or the elementary school student who stumped his classmates in Hangman by learning a list of words without vowels. (I vividly recall his look of glee as students tried vowel after vowel, trying to guess "rhythms" or "cyst.")

At the heart of this efficiency is a facility for spotting the key sub-skill in a particular ability. When I ask coaches, trainers, and high-level performers about this phenomenon they are usually quick to identify what that might be in their field of endeavor:

- The "Two Card Lift" for close-up magicians
- Learning the mother sauces in French cooking
- The crossover dribble in basketball
- Using free indirect style for writing literary fiction

- The cascade pattern in juggling
- Double clutching for driving a manual truck
- The back corner shot in squash
- A Gladwell-style anecdotal analogy in popular social-science nonfiction

What links these disparate skills together is that they are inflection points for achieving mastery in that particular field; being able to make a habit of these skills opens up an array of other potential techniques and learning, whereas not being able to apply these skills in a routine way can significantly hamper your development.

Charles Duhigg (2014) calls these subtle but influential changes of practice "keystone habits." He argues that you don't have to focus on changing every aspect of what you do to bring about personal and organizational change, but rather, concentrate on "identifying a few key priorities and fashioning them into powerful levers" (p. 101). Duhigg suggests we should target "the habits that matter most . . . the ones that, when they start to shift, dislodge and remake other patterns" (p. 101). Another researcher in the field of habit acquisition, James Clear (2018), makes a similar case for focusing on what he calls "atomic habits"—"little habits that are part of a larger system . . . [they are] not only small and easy to do, but also the source of incredible power" (p. 27).

There are routines and techniques in teaching that function like these keystone or atomic habits in being small changes that can make a powerful difference—they are "tipping points" for significant change. The Simple Shifts outlined here—these "tipping points"—both represent the threshold point for entry into a new system of practice (they are small changes that are quick to adopt), and act as the catalyst for further change (they represent a change in mind frame).

There is a wealth of information on best practice for teachers, with new studies and the changing needs of schools and students guaranteeing that teachers will never be short on advice for how to optimize their practice. But how much of that can teachers actually take on? How does anyone manage to navigate the plethora of recommended techniques, habits, skills, and practices that teachers are presented with? By focusing on the few skills that matter.

The Simple Shifts that I describe in this book are relatively easy to implement, but are skills that "have the power to start a chain reaction" (Duhigg, 2014, p. 100). They are emblematic of deeper perspective shifts, and thus, when you start to use them, they begin to change not just how your students respond in your classes, but how you view your role as a teacher. A small change like increasing your wait time when asking questions—the Simple Shift we explore in Shift 4: Wait Time—not only has an immediate effect on the response your students give, but begins to focus your practice on eliciting feedback from students, exploring what they are thinking, and encouraging a culture of "thinking out loud" in the classroom rather than getting the answer right.

Research on implementing a change in practice or behavior confirms that choosing a few pivotal skills to work on—skills that are discrete, manageable, and measurable—is the best way to bring about major change. But the further benefits of this approach are obvious within the teaching context—with such a time-intensive, demanding job, you need the most effective use of your limited time to gain the greatest effect. Simple Shifts can offer you that.

So what are the Simple Shifts for teachers?

- **Low-Key Interventions**—"Nudging" students back to their work when they are exhibiting off-task behavior
- **Pivoting and Reframing**—Pivoting around students' argumentative responses, defusing conflict, and steering them back to their learning
- **Instructional Clarity**—Securing complete student attention before issuing instructions or making transitions
- **Wait Time**—Extending the amount of thinking time you give your students *before* expecting them to respond to questions
- **Pause and Elaboration Time**—Extending the length of time you pause *after* your students answer to encourage them to elaborate
- **Snapshot Feedback**—Using fast, formative feedback from your students to assess the immediate impact of your teaching
- **Reflection Time**—Giving students an opportunity to quickly *demonstrate* that they have taken on your advice

Of course, there are many other foundational skills that have the potential to effect a similarly significant change, but these were chosen for their ease of implementation. No matter how transformative a new teaching technique might be, if it is difficult or time-consuming to implement, the chances are that you will never see its effect. Being "small and easy to do" is a crucial part of what makes Simple Shifts so effective.

Micro-data tools

In the Introduction, I asked what a Fitbit for teachers would look like. My answer to this question is: micro-data tools. Micro-data tools can be an essential part of the "how" of changing teaching practice.

Micro-data tools allow you to record data on specific aspects of your classroom practice. These tools can take many forms—tally chart, checklist, annotated student roll, classroom map, timesheet—but essentially they focus on one or two teaching techniques or student behaviors and provide you with a way to monitor your progress as you adopt new teaching routines.

The reason these tools are labeled as *micro*-data is to distinguish them from all the other data we collect as schools and teachers. Much of this data—diagnostic literacy and numeracy testing, end-of-year exams, system-level assessments—is collected annually or over term and semester cycles. Even in schools where I work that have a keen interest in gathering data to help refine teacher practice, much of the data they collect—pre- and post-topic test results and monthly student surveys, for example—is taken every few weeks. This information is essential for reviewing student growth and school and district performance, but it is not as useful for a teacher trying to establish a new teaching routine or skill. For that, what is required is a habit tracker—a tool for monitoring your progress with a much shorter feedback loop. This kind of tool allows you to take daily or lesson-by-lesson data about the new practice you are trying to establish.

Each of the seven Simple Shifts in this book has been paired with a number of micro-data tools. These tools measure some aspect of teacher or student behavior that is associated with using that Simple Shift successfully. The tools give you quick, indicative measures of performance that both remind you to employ this strategy and give you fast feedback about its effect.

Have a look at this example from the chapter on Instructional Clarity:

MICRO-DATA TOOL	
Verbal vs. Nonverbal Interventions Tally	
Verbal reminders What do you say to the group and individual students to keep them on task?	**Nonverbal reminders** How do you remind students to maintain their attention without having to interrupt what you are saying?
⩘⩘ ⩘⩘ |||	||||
TOTAL:	**TOTAL:**

This tool records the number of times the teacher had to speak to get their students back on task. It also records the total number of instances where the teacher was able to steer their students back to the task using a nonverbal technique such as a hand signal or facial expression.

The golden rule of addressing low-level off-task behavior is finding the lowest level of intervention that works (we explore this in Shift One: Low-Key Interventions). Being aware of how you use verbal and nonverbal interventions is a good way then to ensure that you are looking at the breadth of options available in these situations, and employing this tally helps you do that. Moreover, if you are working on using more nonverbal interventions—using more proximity reminders, for example—then this data tool can be used to prompt you to both employ this strategy and record the *frequency* with which you use it.

What makes micro-data tools effective?

Changing practice is not easy. From our own experience as teachers, and from research into behavior change and habit acquisition, we know that *wanting* to change and *enacting* that change are two very different things. In fact, the research is very clear that in many fields of endeavor, *resolving* to do something does not result in a person exhibiting that behavior in even *30 percent* of cases (Sheerhan, 2002). What we think of as "willpower" and "self-discipline" are vastly overrated. Making small changes, becoming conscious of our habits, getting regular feedback, and tracking success are all far better indicators of successful routine development. I think this is a seminal point: Skill development and routine behavior change is not a question of *character* or *will*, but knowing and planning precisely how you will bring about the change you seek.

And this is sometimes what books about teaching don't foreground (or even acknowledge)—it takes effort to carry a new learning into action. As with students, when I'm coaching teachers I want to give them not just the reasons to adopt new practice, but the mechanism by which they can do that. This book is an effort to give teachers not just the *why* of new teaching practice, but the *how*.

In *Atomic Habits*, Clear argues that to reach our objectives, focusing on *goals* is less effective than focusing on *systems*. This is another way of understanding how important the "how" of practice change is—knowing where you want to go is ultimately not as important as having a specific plan of how you are going to get there. "Systems are about the processes that lead to [those] results. . . . You do not rise to the level of your goals. You fall to the level of your systems" (pp. 23, 27).

Micro-data tools offer a simple system for managing practice change. They enable you to be conscious of your existing habits, they demand a small, specific change rather than an amorphous intention, they monitor your progress toward your goal, and they provide nonattributive feedback (feedback without judgment). Let's look at each of these in more detail.

Making habits conscious

Like driving a car, much of what we do when teaching becomes automatic. While lesson and curriculum planning, correcting written work, and other elements of teaching require higher-order skills that engage the conscious mind, many parts of day-to-day classroom regulation and student interaction happen automatically. Our effectiveness as teachers hinges on how we navigate the classroom environment: how we guide and shape discussion, how we respond to interruptions and unproductive behavior, and how we assess what our students know and instruct them how to proceed next. Our habits for dealing with these situations, then, are enormously important in shaping our ultimate outcomes.

Routines and habits are a way for the human brain to shortcut its processes. Our brains are exceedingly complex and, within the economy of the body, very expensive to run. So many things demand attention, and require a decision, assessment, or solution, that the brain tries to streamline how much effort is involved in each of these. Where possible, the brain seeks patterns, shortcuts, and quick, generalized solutions that require less conscious thinking time (Duhigg, 2014).

One of the most important insights we can take from the research into habits is that for us to exert any control over our habits—to create or change them—they must first become conscious. We need to be aware of what we are doing, and what the ultimate effect of that response or behavior is. In the chapters that follow, we will explore in detail how each of the Simple Shifts changes your students' experience of learning, and why they are effective skills to develop. In the process, you will be able to examine your current teaching routines, and to think critically about aspects of your teaching that you might not ordinarily notice (Clear, 2018).

Identifying and labeling a specific skill using a micro-data tool makes you more conscious about this aspect of your practice. This doesn't just apply to those who are learning a skill. Many able and experienced teachers have a high degree of automaticity—some of the subtle techniques in their teaching have become so "second nature" they aren't even aware any more of using them. Labeling these techniques helps give you a conscious awareness of what you are doing and therefore makes it more likely you will be willing and able to pass on these ideas to others.

Tracking works

One significant way we can close the gap between what we resolve to do ("goal intention") and our objectives ("goal attainment") is to monitor our progress. Progress monitoring has a significant impact on goal attainment, making you more likely to both strive for and meet your goals (Harkin et al., 2016). Micro-data tools make it easy for you to track your progress toward your teaching goals.

Merely tracking—with no specific intention to increase or decrease the incidence of the behavior being tracked—has been shown to have an impact on how people act. Monitoring or measuring is a regular reminder, and keeps the behavior change in your conscious mind. But tracking also has the advantage of making the new skill compelling to do.

My colleague's Fitbit is a perfect example of a simple mechanism that made him want to get those 10,000 steps each day. Having a daily total on his wrist is a constant reminder of his goal, and the buzzing when he achieves it is a small but nevertheless attractive reward that motivates him to keep walking. A simple nudge like this one is surprisingly effective at keeping people on track.

One of the reasons for this is that a tracking device with incremental goals and rewards taps into our strong underlying capacity for learning through reinforcement. Our minds are primed for reinforcement—from an evolutionary perspective, it's the way we learn which behaviors to repeat and which to avoid.

Instant feedback, the kind we get from micro-data tools, is a potent reward for our brain, and generates the kind of feedback loop that underlies all automatic behavior. So tracking our progress is a simple way to work *with* our brains to make a behavior more compelling, and thus embed it as a new routine skill.

Quick, simple, and concrete

Another insight from habit research is that in order to make a new behavior stick, we need to focus on small, easy, and specific changes. That is, we need to avoid vague intentions and instead aim for concrete, attainable actions that can be clearly recognized when we have achieved them.

Clear (2018) argues that new habits or practices should be easy enough to complete quickly. "Even when you know you should start small, it's easy to start big," he states, which makes the change that much harder to both start and continue (p. 162). He argues we should view these new skills as "gateway habits"—small changes that are easy to do, but open the door on a cascade of other improvements that flow from this simple step.

You can see from the example on page 5 that using a micro-data tool is a straightforward process. Typically, all it requires is for the observer to put tally marks into a couple of columns or mark data on a simple map or grid throughout the lesson. If doing this *and* teaching at the same time seems difficult, you could try videotaping part of a lesson and reviewing it using the tool, or finding a peer partner to take the data for you. Because the tool is so simple to use, almost anyone can do this kind of recording—you can give a colleague relatively short notice and they will quickly pick it up. Indeed, I have occasionally asked student teachers, or even students, to take this data for me. (A colleague I know who often gets his students to take this data for him has a rule of thumb for selecting students to do this: "Just pick the kid who *already* gives you extensive feedback about your performance.") In each case, these people have quickly grasped what is required of them.

Part of the simplicity of micro-data tools is that they are narrowly focused on just one or two aspects of practice. The narrow focus of micro-data tools also means that any classroom observation is a less stressful process. If you are doing the observing, you know precisely what to look for. Instead of having to give general feedback about your peer partner's performance, you are simply recording data on their chosen target. Anyone who has taken this data will know that it is hard to concentrate on anything going on in the room but the nominated data point, as you are so focused on this one element of their practice.

Similarly, if you are being observed you don't have to worry about your colleague noting or giving you feedback about those unrepresentative moments that might occur in the lesson, as they are exclusively focused on a single element of your practice.

Micro-data tools encourage nonattributive feedback

Schools often draw a distinction between giving positive and negative feedback. However, when it comes to habit change, I think it is more useful to distinguish between attributive and nonattributive feedback.

When someone gives you feedback it can involve a subtle level of presumption. The person giving it is implicitly accepting that they are in a position to say: "This is what you are like." We call this *attribution*.

In my experience, teachers are often uncomfortable with attributive feedback. This is not just concern about receiving negative feedback, but a more general discomfort about being *judged* in the first place. Note how many teachers balk at even low-level praise from their colleagues. This might sometimes seem like self-deprecation or false modesty, but I think there is an element of unease with the subtle power dynamics of having your behavior evaluated by someone else—even in a positive way.

I coach school teams to move away from this attributive approach and instead offer each other nonattributive feedback (Kegan & Lahey, 2012). Rather than telling someone how well they did, you tell them about your *experience* of their actions. That is, you just describe what you observed without the presumption of telling them what this experience means about them. This is not "you are" but "I noticed" feedback. Some examples:

- **Attributive:** *You are so good at getting students to take part in the discussion.*
- **Nonattributive:** *I saw that 13 different students offered an answer during the discussion.*

Nonattributive feedback is effective because it gives you data about your teaching without offering judgments about you as a teacher. Instead of feeling the need to immediately correct this feedback because it doesn't fit your sense (good or bad) of yourself, it prompts you to take your time to reflect deeply on your practice.

Micro-data tools are nonattributive. In the example above, the observer is noting data with dashes or dots—not ticks and crosses. Presented with this data by a colleague or having recorded it yourself, you have a starting point for thinking about a specific teaching technique without having to feel judged as you work toward making it a more routine part of your practice.

The Simple Shifts featured in this book give you an efficient way of improving your teaching practice, and micro-data tools that both prompt and monitor this change.

So what might this look like? In the next chapters, we explore practical ways to put the Simple Shifts into action.

Shift One: Low-Key Interventions

"Nudging" students back to their work when they are exhibiting off-task behavior

Teachers often have to address off-task behavior. This doesn't have to be malicious or aggressive conduct—it might just be that your students are distracted or unfocused. Talking out of turn, wandering around the room, annoying a classmate, being glacially slow to start work, or just not staying on task are classic examples of low-level, off-task behavior. And though these behaviors are fairly minor infractions, they can nonetheless stop individual students or even whole classes from making the most of your teaching and their learning.

Whether you are in a school with highly compliant classes where the odd student might need to be steered back to the learning, or a school where the behavior is challenging and you want to reduce the amount of low-level, off-task distractions (so you can concentrate on more extreme behaviors), you need strategies for addressing these behaviors.

The key principle for addressing low-level, off-task behavior is finding the lowest-level possible intervention that works. This can be difficult. A couple of years ago, I observed a middle-school class where the teacher deftly dealt with distraction after distraction. Despite the high volume of interruptions, she was able to keep her students on-task with lots of verbal commands.

Here is a transcript of just 40 seconds of that class:

> *Andre, put that down. Stephanie, put that away. No, you can do that later. Get back to it, you two. Kyle, open your laptop and get started. You too, Demarcus. Not in here, guys. Uh, I don't think so. Ellie, no. No!*

It was an impressive effort and one that was effective in keeping the students focused on their history task. However, when I visited the same class the next day, the teacher had to say exactly the same things to the same students. You don't want to expend all of your energy on monitoring your students' behavior—you want to build a culture where as much of your time as possible is spent on the learning.

Mastering low-key interventions helps you meet this goal. If you can guide a student back toward their learning without having to say anything, you can continue with your instruction uninterrupted. Low-key interventions can be quite subtle, and I find with teachers I am coaching that it is easier to first model the approach than to explain why they work. So what do low-key interventions look like?

Let's start with an example of off-task behavior: Tayah is slow to start her work and keeps interrupting her table partner. The mistake that I see all the time with addressing this kind of behavior is that teachers give it more attention than it deserves. Many teachers in this situation will interrupt the lesson to call out to Tayah, or approach her desk and address her one-on-one. This may solve the problem in a single instance, but in the longer term it is problematic. Giving this kind of attention to ensure compliance can often habituate the student to get back on task *only* when the teacher has spoken to them, and can even lead to students who won't get underway until the teacher has checked in with them individually.

The key to dealing with these behaviors is making sure you use the lowest level possible intervention. In these situations, I encourage teachers to try the following strategies.

On-task praise

Probably the lowest-key teacher intervention is to simply praise students who are doing the right thing. "Catch your kids behaving" is a golden rule of creating a positive culture in your classroom. When you acknowledge students who are on task, you are also reminding students who are slow to start or who are distracted to get back to their work.

So in the example above, rather than immediately approaching Tayah about her behavior, you might seek out those students who are engaged with their study and acknowledge their efforts:

> *I can see the group at the back are underway.*
> *Kiama has already highlighted the question sheet.*
> *Reuben has started.*
> *Devin is already up to question two.*

When I'm working with teachers who want to build their class's independence, I suggest an even more targeted approach: Praise not only the students who are on task but those who specifically demonstrate self-regulation.

> *Great persistence, Matt.*
> *I like that you chose to avoid those distractions, Nikki.*
> *Good decision to find something else to go on with once you were finished, Sue.*

Why does this approach work? There are two clear reasons why this approach is effective for dealing with low-level, off-task behavior.

On-task praise shapes class culture

A fundamental rule of behavior change is that "what is rewarded is repeated" (Clear, 2018, p. 86). On-task praise is a clear signal about what you value in your classes. Praise the work habits you are trying to cultivate, and you will, over time, see more of them (Moore et al., 2010). Encouraging your students to demonstrate these behaviors builds a positive culture that helps "crowd out" off-task behavior—or at least reduce the time and energy devoted to it in your classroom.

On-task praise is subtle

It is the indirect nature of this strategy that makes it so appealing: You prompt students about what is required of them without having to specifically address them. Praising a classmate for being on task reminds the distracted student that she should be working too. This is effective in nearly a quarter of cases in my video coaching of teachers. Indeed, not only do they see this approach routinely working with the students they are targeting, they often see it altering the behavior of other students as well. "Look at that," a teacher noted to me in a video coaching session. "I was trying to get Josh back to work and I got Kim as well—a two for one bonus!"

Of course, this approach doesn't work every time for every student. Moreover, some teachers I encounter are uncomfortable with using on-task praise. Here are the major reservations I hear from these teachers:

It is (or should be) unnecessary. Many teachers feel that acknowledging students who are doing the right thing is unnecessary: "Why should I thank a student for something they should be doing anyway?" During a workshop on building positive behaviors, one teacher put it to me this way: "I don't go in for that warm and fuzzy stuff—I just tell it like it is." This teacher's choice of language here is telling—he felt like focusing on the positive meant that he wouldn't be addressing the reality of the situation. I would argue the opposite: Responding mainly to off-task behaviors ignores the basic reality that many students routinely do the right thing, and as a result, get less attention. Compliant students should not get substantially less teacher support than those who need extra direction. At the very least, we should create a culture that recognizes students when they are working hard.

If you don't find this argument persuasive, you might try drawing a distinction between "praise" and "acknowledgment" (Lemov, 2015, pp. 435–436). When I am coaching teachers who have reservations about using on-task praise, I use Lemov's work to differentiate between acknowledgment and praise:

- **Acknowledgment** is when you recognize when a student meets your expectations.
- **Praise** is an acknowledgment for exceeding your expectations. (I sometimes label praise "approval" here to avoid confusion with on-task praise.)

By focusing on the students who have earned Lemov's idea of praise—those who are working above your expectations—you can trial on-task praise while sticking with an approach with which you are comfortable.

It is inauthentic. The other common concern raised about on-task praise is that it is not authentic, but merely an empty gesture that has little impact on the students. "My kids don't like fake praise," one senior science teacher told me, "any more than I like listening to generic thank-yous to staff from leadership at the end of the school year." The teacher here is being sarcastic but is highlighting a key issue: The type of praise you give does matter. Vague, formulaic feedback (like "Well done, everyone—your work is good") can ring hollow.

To avoid this trap, you should endeavor to make your feedback direct, specific, and nonattributive (Kegan & Lahey, 2012):

- **Direct:** Address your comments specifically to the students doing the right thing—they deserve the personal acknowledgment.
- **Specific:** Avoid generic feedback and be explicit about what the student is doing successfully. The more concrete you are, the easier it is for other students to mirror these behaviors.
- **Nonattributive:** Describe your own experience of what the student is doing (*I noticed the way Michael checked his draft against the criteria*) rather than characterize what the student is like (*Michael is really good at drafting his work properly*).

This does not always apply in every interaction with a student. However, I have found in my own teaching that where I can use it, nonattributive feedback has a positive effect. Firstly, students are more likely to accept praise—after all, you are not passing judgment on who they are, merely stating what you have observed. Secondly, by emphasizing what your student did successfully (instead of saying that they are successful), you are emphasizing their effort over their ability. This tallies with the final advantage of this approach: Students find it easier to reproduce behavior that is successful when the teacher is describing the behavior, not the person.

These concerns with on-task praise are worth addressing because such a simple habit can be transformative. When it comes to "nudging" students to focus on their work or building a positive classroom culture, on-task praise can utterly change how you approach low-level, off-task behavior. Fundamentally, it helps you get into the mindset of building on what students are already doing well ("scaling successes") rather than addressing problems. Or as I put it to teachers in coaching sessions: When it comes to encouraging positive behavior in the classroom, it is not what you say "No" to but what you say "Yes" to that counts.

Does this mean that our off-task student, Tayah, is now definitely back on task?

Hardly.

On-task praise will reduce the volume and frequency of students who are off task, but teachers need a range of other low-key interventions when this approach doesn't work.

Proximity without eye contact

We noted before that when a student is off task, a teacher's natural impulse is to call out to the student or work with them one-on-one to get them back on track. The danger is that they will come to expect this help and not develop the personal initiative to self-regulate their behavior. Using proximity to nudge your students back on track but withholding eye contact is a balanced way to use your influence without reducing the student's independence.

To use this technique, you start by approaching Tayah and standing beside her, about an arm's length away—it is important that you are not standing too close as this can be intimidating. Without looking at her directly, you then survey the class, using your proximity to cue her to get back to work. You will often see students glance up at you or down at their work at this moment—indicating that they are aware of your presence and realize they need to get back to work. If Tayah has no reaction and continues with her off-task behavior, don't immediately abandon the strategy. Instead, change your position. Rather than move closer, move backwards a half step so that now you are standing at a 45-degree angle to her on the edge of her peripheral vision. Again, without looking at Tayah directly, you watch carefully to see if your proximity has nudged her back on task. I often train teachers to reset at this moment—move to another part of the classroom from where they can subtly monitor to see if the strategy has worked.

Using proximity in this way can be effective for all sorts of situations, but one particular response tends to flummox teachers. I get a lot of questions in workshops about what to do if the student turns in your direction and starts addressing you: A loud "Hello!" or "Why are you standing there?" are common examples. The response is fairly straightforward. If some of your students are responding in this way, just add one further step to this technique: Before you approach the student who is off task, identify one of their classmates who is working well, noting where they are up to in their work. Then if Tayah tries to get your attention, you can simply step away from the interaction while addressing that other student:

Chris, are you up to question six already?

By moving away from Tayah, you stymie her efforts to engage you in a conversation, and talking while you do this means that you aren't snubbing her (avoiding an aggrieved "OK ignore me then!"-style response) so much as engaging another student. The key here is watching Tayah's movements closely and initiating this response the moment you get a sign—she starts to turn her head or open her mouth—that she is going to interact with you, and immediately moving toward the other student.

This proximity technique has two clear impacts on your teaching:

Using proximity heightens your awareness. Using this subtle technique makes you more aware of how minor changes of practice can shape student behavior. When you see how something as simple as withholding or adding eye contact changes how your students behave, it makes you more likely to try other subtle adjustments of practice. At two schools where I run video coaching programs, for example, it was studying how teachers use proximity that led teachers to adopt a cascade of other teaching techniques. They found that using proximity to guide students toward the right behavior—and seeing this succeed—made them more deliberate about all the little things they did in class.

Using proximity heightens your sense of agency. Moreover, this strategy helps you concentrate your attention on the aspects of the situation over which you have control. Off-task behavior—even low-level off-task behavior—can make teachers feel powerless. Focusing your attention on the subtleties of your own practice can give you a greater sense of agency: We don't have total control over our students, but we have complete control over ourselves.

Of course, this does not mean using proximity without eye contact will always work. No single behavioral intervention does. But it will help you reduce the total number of distractions you have to address verbally.

Cross praise

This technique is a targeted version of on-task praise. Typically, it involves praising students *near* an off-task student with the express purpose of reminding them what they should be doing. The key to this technique is positioning yourself so that your praise passes across the off-task student, subtly including them within your conversation. The importance of positioning is implicit in its name and in other labels (parallel cueing, parallel acknowledgment) given to this technique.

In my experience, cross praise is one of the most effective low-key techniques for getting students back to work. It is also one of the most under-utilized. Where then might you use it? Let's go back to the situation with Tayah: We have tried general praise and using proximity but neither strategy seems to have gotten her back to work. Cross praise is the obvious next step. As with proximity, your first move is to position yourself near Tayah. Take care to ensure you have positioned yourself in such a way that discussion with Tayah's classmates takes place with her between you and the student or students you are addressing. The rule of thumb when coaching someone to adopt this technique is: Don't stand in the student's personal space but make sure your comments pass through it.

The type of praise you deliver here is nearly the same as those with other forms of on-task praise. However, with other forms of on-task praise we often use what is called narration (Lemov, 2015) where we comment out loud to the rest of the class about a specific individual's performance:

I can see that Linda has started her work.

When using cross praise, you directly address the student:

I can see you have started, Linda.

Now watch the off-task student through the periphery of your vision: Does their body language or expression suggest they have noted your comments? Do they look toward the student you are talking to? Or up at you? Do they look at their work, start typing or pick up a pen? If any of these occur, reset your position and see if this reminder has been enough to send Tayah back to her work.

The appeal of cross praise is twofold:

Cross praise is versatile. You can use cross praise in lots of different situations. For instance, you don't need the students you are praising to always be in the immediate vicinity of the off-task student. As long as you are close enough to the student who is off task that they feel implicated in your conversation, the other students you are speaking to can be right across the room. I have seen cross praise used effectively in large open classrooms, across playing fields, and in small-group reading sessions.

Cross praise is subtle. You can use this technique without your students even noticing. I once conducted a workshop on developing positive behaviors with an ex-student in attendance. After the session, he approached me to say he enjoyed the workshop but wasn't sure that cross praise would work. When I mentioned that I used it with him every single class over a two-year period he laughed—he thought I was joking. I had to reiterate before he believed me: "You are probably the most cross-praised student in Australia!" I think it is telling that even a person who had studied the technique, seen it modeled, and experienced it regularly as a student was still unsure it would work. Cross praise is a good example of a small, almost unnoticeable change of practice that can nonetheless change student behavior.

If cross praise doesn't work, this might be the time to shift to a verbal intervention with Tayah. I think one of the best first options is just naming the behavior you want from the student: "We are working on question six, getting started, thanks" seems to work better than "Stop mucking around and distracting others." The other effective first option is to use a micro-command—a short, sharp directive that you would typically employ if the behavior was more problematic. I have found "Not here," "Inappropriate time," or "Back to it" are all effective in this situation. It is important to have these next steps in my mind because cross praise will not always work. As with proximity, though, it will reduce the total number of times you will have to break from instruction to talk with students about getting back on task.

Micro-data tools: Tracking low-key interventions

There are lots of ways to record the use of low-key interventions in your classroom. One of the easiest is to track the way you use praise.

Affirmations vs. Commands Chart: This micro-data tool, as shown on page 20, records the number of times you praise students to shape their behavior (which you mark in the left-hand column), and the number of times you have to instruct them on what to do (which is placed in the right).

MICRO-DATA TOOL

Affirmations vs. Commands Chart

Affirmations	Commands
Any time you acknowledge success or endorse behavior.	Any time you tell a student what to do, give instructions, or challenge off-task behaviors.
"That was a fast transition guys. Excellent."	*"Everyone get in pairs and then line up against the wall."*
"Have a look at Li's answer here—this is how this question should be approached. . . ."	*"Everyone, please look this way."*
"I can see that you asked three people before you asked me. Good use of initiative."	*"Come here. You are not to speak to me like that again. Is that understood?"*
"This group alerted others to the rallying call.* Well done."	*"Stop it, Michael. That is not appropriate."*

* See Shift Three for more on rallying calls.

It is important to remember that we're not suggesting affirmations are good and commands bad. The praise must be "contingent on or as a consequence of appropriate student behavior" (Partin et al., 2010, p. 173). Students see through empty praise and being positive about poor behavior can be disastrous. There are many situations where instruction is required—when we teach very young students a high percentage of instruction needs to be explicit commands. (The first time I taught a class of five-year-olds, I asked a boy, "Would you come over here?" His response was a pithy "No.")

Rather than judge our interventions as right or wrong, this micro-data tool is designed to make us more conscious of how we use praise and commands in the classroom. When you are analyzing this data, you should try to avoid assessing whether you reached a *particular number* of affirmations or commands. Instead, I get teachers to focus on how *deliberately* they used these strategies. The best coaching question to ask yourself here is: "Was the ratio of affirmations to commands what I intended?" This question helps you reflect on whether you used affirmations and commands in a targeted way, or defaulted into a reactive response to student behavior. If you are thinking about using this micro-data tool, plan to use it at least two or three times per month or term. Repeating this process helps grow your awareness of how you are using commands and affirmations and allows you to compare and contrast data between lessons as you build this awareness.

Affirmations vs. Commands App: The app version of this tool, which is available at mcrel.org/tiltingyourteaching, is similarly simple to use. As with most micro-data tools, it works well if a peer partner or instructional coach takes the data for you or if you review the lesson on video. However, because of the tool's simplicity, I have found it effective to use it myself during class—an approach that heightens your real-time awareness of how you employ praise.

Verbal vs. Nonverbal Interventions Tally: Alternatively, you might try the Verbal vs. Nonverbal Interventions Tally data tool we introduced in the last chapter. Both the paper tally version and the app version are effective mechanisms for noting the frequency with which you use strategies such as on-task praise, proximity, and parallel cueing.

Time on Task Tool: One other approach you might try is a Time on Task tool. Jim Knight (2018) advises doing this by using a seating chart and, at intervals determined by a timer, recording on the chart whether each student is on or off task. I have found that marking a horizontal (off task) or vertical (on task) line next to each student's spot on the seating chart is a quick way to do this. The Time on Task tool gives you a clear snapshot of who is doing what is asked of them and who is not. Moreover, marking this data on a seating chart means you can see the *pattern* of behavior across your class and identify blind spots where pockets of off-task behavior might require a bit more dedicated attention.

Experience Sampling Tool: Some of the schools I have worked with are reluctant to use the Time on Task approach because it doesn't differentiate between students who are engaged and those who are merely being compliant. If you want to use low-key interventions to boost not just compliance but engagement, you might try an Experience Sampling tool to poll your students about their level of interest. To do this, you simply set a timer and when it goes off, your students have to record on a sheet their level of engagement from noncompliant through compliant to engaged (Knight, 2018). In my own class, I trialed these as traffic light rankings: Green (*I'm into it*), Amber (*I'm doing it*), and Red (*I'm over it*). It was an approach that worked really well in giving me a sense of how genuinely engaged students were—albeit in intervals—over the course of my lesson.

I worked with a teacher-leader who saw me model this technique at his school and adopted it when he ran a staff meeting to gauge his audience's engagement. I liked his description of the data he received—he found it both instructive *and* disheartening. If you are employing this tool for the first time, it is worth recognizing that sometimes the engagement data you receive from this tool might be like this. Don't be demoralized. Just treat this data as a benchmark and see if this changes as you get better at quickly steering students away from off-task behavior and are able to put more of your time to engaging students with their learning.

The range of effective methods for recording off-task behavior means you can vary which data tool you use depending on whether you want to target a particular intervention (for example, Affirmation vs. Commands for on-task praise or Nonverbal vs. Verbal for proximity) or look more generally at the effect of using these techniques on compliance and engagement.

Summing up

These low-key interventions are not meant to completely supplant your usual methods of dealing with off-task behavior. Rather, they are meant to get you thinking about your default strategies: Could you employ one or two of these alternatives before you use the interventions you normally employ? This requires thinking about your instinctive responses. Dealing with off-task behavior is usually habitual: Asking a student to get back to work is something you would do many times a day. Changing these "rusted on" patterns can take some effort.

You might find it useful to think about what kicks off your routine response. Routines are usually initiated by a "cue"—a trigger that starts your move into automatic behavior. The research on habit acquisition tells us that while it's hard to eliminate an old routine—cues are really hard to resist once they are hardwired into your brain—it *is* possible to replace one routine with another. "You must keep the old cue but insert a new routine," argues Duhigg (2014, p. 62).

If you want to use more low-key interventions, think about the student behaviors that cue your responses in class. Is it a student talking out of turn that makes you respond with a verbal reminder? Is it a group being slow to start that makes you go and stand at their desk and explain again what is required of them? Identify the cues that kick off the routine response you want to change, and then plan ahead what new routine you want to try instead. (*The next time Sunil is distracted, rather than telling him off, I'm going to see if using proximity without eye contact gets him back on task.*) Try and be very specific about your plans to put this new routine into action. It tends to work best if you nominate where and when you are going to use it and what cue will initiate this routine:

> *I'm in room 602 for period four tomorrow. I'm going to try using proximity without eye contact whenever students chat instead of working.*

This type of planning is called an "implementation intention" and it increases the chances that you make these new practices into new habits (Gollwitzer, 1999).

In the midst of a busy lesson it's hard not to default to your existing habits, so a bit of planning goes a long way to trying strategies like on-task praise, proximity with eye contact, and cross praise. But I have found time and again that low-key interventions quickly become habits: Among the teachers I coach, the take-up rate is high once they have successfully used these techniques. This is because of the powerful feedback you get: Every time you successfully use one of these strategies you change your students' behavior in a low-key way that makes it easier to preserve your relationship with them. And better relationships, of course, mean better learning—and less wear and tear on *everyone* in the classroom.

Shift Two: Pivoting and Reframing

Pivoting around students' argumentative responses, defusing conflict, and steering them back to their learning

When students are being unnecessarily argumentative, pivot around their arguments and back to the real issue—their learning.

In my very first week of teaching I had a run-in with a student who threw a rock at the whiteboard in my classroom. After I reacted with some yelling and aggressive body language (an ideal response to defuse the situation), I demanded that the student explain why he threw the rock. Of course, I can now see this as a rookie mistake. What did I expect him to say . . . "I was exhibiting some classic adolescent risk-taking behavior in the form of an attention-seeking disruption. I think I was wanting to gain social status by testing the boundaries of acceptable classroom behavior. Sorry, it won't happen again"?

His response was, in fact, much cleverer than that:

It wasn't a rock—it was a stone!

As an experienced teacher, I know the appropriate way to deal with this sort of response is to skirt around this argument and address the issue at hand—his dangerous behavior. Instead I said, "It *is* a rock! It's, like, six-and-half centimeters in circumference!"

The moment the comment left my mouth, I had a sudden perception switch and I could hear what I sounded like through the thin partition wall to the teacher next door, as I argued how small a rock should be before you can throw it at your teacher.

I was deeply embarrassed.

Since then, I have largely managed to avoid becoming entangled in such farcical exchanges in my classes. However, I would be lying if I said I'd never been sidetracked in an argument when trying to deal with a student's off-task behavior. It is inevitable that young people will test your authority as they develop their own sense of personal autonomy. Arguing with authority figures such as teachers, parents, and guardians is a normal part of development for many adolescents. The key for dealing with this behavior in your classroom is anticipating it and planning how you intend to respond. This is a golden rule of teaching: "Students are going to misbehave as they learn and grow—it's how we respond to their misbehavior that matters" (D. Smith et al., 2015, p. 3).

So how do we deal with students who argue and resist? The Simple Shift here is using a pivot phrase.

Pivot phrases

Pivot phrases are carefully worded responses that you can use to avoid arguments and redirect students back to their learning. They are sometimes referred to as "micro scripts" (Dix, 2017), a label which describes their role well: They are rehearsed responses that lay out the precise language you can use to address a student who is being argumentative.

> **Reminder:** *Sit down, thanks, Lee.*
>
> **Resistance** (pointing to a classmate): *That's not fair—he's standing up!*
>
> **Pivot:** *Nevertheless, sit down, thank you.*

I often tell teachers whom I coach that while students sometimes plan how they misbehave, they rarely plan how to argue with teachers when that behavior is addressed. ("Being angry and reactive today didn't work, so maybe I should just be apathetic tomorrow?") However, teachers *can* plan in advance and this should give you a big advantage in dealing with these behaviors.

Sometimes when I am modeling how to address argumentative students, teachers will compliment me for the quick way I responded to a particular student: "I would never be able to think of that on the spot!" They always seem relieved when I tell them: "Neither would I." The best impromptu statements in classroom management often aren't. Planning out and practicing how you might respond to specific incidences of student resistance means that when they occur in your class you can, on the spur of the moment, respond to them in a well-rehearsed and confident manner.

Following is a range of pivot phrases that you can use to do this. I have grouped them into four categories to better illustrate how they work, but in practice you will probably use multiple pivots from different categories in a single encounter with a student. You can also use them as examples to create your own versions that feel right for you. What matters most is that they become familiar enough for you to quickly employ in an intuitive way when you meet with student resistance.

> ### Contextualizing Pivot Phrases
>
> Before we look at a whole range of pivot phrases, it is important to establish where pivot phrases sit within the wider framework of how you are expected to respond to off-task behavior in your school. Most schools have well-defined expectations about how students are to act in the classroom—and how teachers are to address behavior that doesn't meet these standards. In your school, this could take many different forms: a clearly laid-out ladder of consequences for off-task behavior, a restorative justice framework, or a list of rights and responsibilities for teacher and students alike.
>
> Pivot phrases are not alternatives to these frameworks, they are strategies you can use to support them. They give you a way to remind students of their responsibilities, to steer them away from behavior for which there are serious consequences and allow you to intervene in situations before they develop into ones that require a restorative process.
>
> Pivot phrases give you the technique to work with greater subtlety within your school's behavioral framework. One of the most common critiques I hear from school leaders is that teachers lean too heavily on these frameworks. Perhaps regarded by teachers as *the* response, rather than a framework to work within when difficult behavior escalates, teachers may implement sanctions against students too readily or initiate formal restorative processes too quickly. Having some practical ways to pivot around student resistance means that you don't need to use these more serious measures so often. Instead you can subtly "nudge" students back toward their learning.

Redirection

When you challenge a student about their behavior, you might not be able to resolve the issue to your satisfaction, but you always get to decide what the issue *is*. That's what makes the example that opens this chapter so laughable. I was ineffective because I let the student dictate what the argument was about—debating the size of the projectile he threw—instead of talking about why throwing it was so dangerous. I accepted the *student's* premise.

The simplest way to avoid this trap is to make clear to your student that the issue they raised is not pertinent to your discussion or up for debate and then pivot immediately back to what you think is the relevant matter.

> **Reminder:** *Finish your work, Sam.*
>
> **Distraction:** *I got all the section B stuff done.*
>
> **Pivot:** *That's not the issue right now. Complete that last question, thank you.*

"That's not the issue right now" is probably the most widely used pivot phrase I see in schools, and the best starting point for making pivoting a habit. First popularized in Australia by Jenny Mackay (2006), it is a great example of a well-honed pivot phrase. In six short words it manages to be both assertive ("that's not the issue") and respectful (it might be an issue at another time but not "right now") and can be employed in a wide range of situations. Over a period of just a few weeks recently, I observed teachers using it successfully in three very different situations.

When a student was seeking to elude responsibility for an action:

> **Student:** *They were mucking around too! Why don't you tell them off?*
>
> **Teacher:** *That's not the issue right now—I'm talking to you.*

When a student was seeking to abruptly change the subject:

> **Student:** *Are you going away, Miss?*
>
> **Teacher:** *That's not the issue right now. Please show me your folder, Matteo.*

When a student was trying to challenge the teacher's legitimacy:

> **Student:** *You're not my real teacher anyway!*
>
> **Teacher:** *That's not the issue right now—follow the school rule, thank you.*

"Nevertheless" is another useful pivot phrase. Its brevity makes it ideal for when a student launches into an extended justification for inappropriate behavior or tries to sidetrack you in some way. The moment your student has even the slightest pause, you can push it into the exchange and pivot straight into your restatement of your expectations.

> **Student:** *I am probably not even going on to do Year 11, so . . .*
>
> **Teacher:** *Nevertheless, you need to meet all of* **this** *class's work requirements.*

You can use "All that being said," "Be that as it may," and "Nonetheless" in a similar fashion.

I picked up my favorite redirection pivot while watching a science teacher teaching robotics. Her middle-school class had filed in for their very first lesson to discover that there was a robot placed on each of their desks. Despite this intriguing prospect, one of them called out in a loud voice: "This is boring!" Clearly, this wasn't a genuine response to the start of the lesson but a test of his new teacher's authority, one that he had probably used (and seen work?) before. What the student didn't anticipate was that the teacher had a response practiced for just this occasion:

> *I welcome feedback, Jose—just not at the start of the lesson. Come and see me at morning tea if you want to chat about whether the class was engaging.*

The student had no response and the lesson continued without interruption.

"How long have you had that one for?" I asked the teacher afterwards. She paused in thought. "Seventeen years . . . I saw a colleague use it once and I have used it ever since."

I have too.

The best way to approach redirection pivots is to try some of these phrases ("This is not open for debate" and "Let's focus on the task" are also worth considering) and see which ones sound and feel natural when you use them in your class.

Reframing

Another way to pivot around student resistance is by redefining how the issue is to be viewed. I often use this approach when a student is attempting to *personalize* an issue. For example, if one of my students is trying to suggest I am unfairly singling them out—rather than just addressing off-task behavior as I would with any other student—I might use a pivot phrase like this:

> **Resistance:** *This is so unfair. Why are you always picking on me?*
>
> **Pivot:** *I'm not talking about* **who** *you are—I'm talking about what you are choosing to do.*

This is a very finely calibrated phrase. It has been carefully worded so that it recasts the encounter in depersonalized terms ("I'm not talking about *who* you are") while still focusing the student's attention on their role in changing this behavior ("I'm talking about what *you are choosing* to do"). There are lots of variations of this pivot and all of them emphasize the student's autonomy in this way. (For example, the last part of the phrase might also sound like this: "I'm talking about how *you decided* to act" or "I'm challenging *you to choose* some more appropriate behavior.")

This careful construction means that this phrase can be employed in many different situations. You can use it in low-key encounters such as when one of your students jokingly claims you are picking on them. Or you can employ it in more serious situations, such as when a student is verbally lashing out in an attempt to use angry explosion to avoid taking responsibility for their own actions.

How else can you use a pivot to reframe a situation? Pivot phrases are useful when issues of fairness come up. Young people often have a keen sense of justice and can be quick to evoke this sense of fairness when arguing with you. This is completely understandable: A growing awareness of their own autonomy and the complexities of social power mean that your students will closely monitor how they and their peers are treated. Am I getting treated the same as everyone else?

However, this sometimes can become an excuse for not taking responsibility for their actions:

Reminder: *Get back to it, thanks, Amir.*

Distraction: *That's so unfair—Shea doesn't even have to do the worksheet!*

This is an example of what we call *external attribution*, where the student seeks to shift the responsibility of their actions onto someone else. This is a popular form of student resistance. For the past 10 years, I have run a professional development program called PD in the Pub. When I poll participants in that course about the most common ways students resist teacher interventions, this blaming of someone else—parent, peer, or even you—is always the audience's number one example. Interestingly, I see this happening frequently in high-performing teachers' classes. I think because these teachers are more likely to differentiate their instruction, there are more overt differences in how the teacher interacts with individual students.

The pivot phrase you can use to address this is:

Reminder: *Get back to it, thanks, Amir.*

Distraction: *That's so unfair—Shea doesn't even have to do the worksheet!*

Reframe: *I am fair to everyone, but I don't treat you identically because you are not identical.*

This is a good example of how challenging the student's underlying presumption allows you to pivot around their argument. The student is confusing evenhandedness with uniformity, and they are not the same thing. Pointing this out allows you to move on quickly from this argument.

Sometimes reframing requires as little effort as just changing a word or a phrase. For example, I often coach new teachers to move from challenging students for "not working" to questioning the students about being "on task." They get far less resistance with this simple shift. Similarly, when you talk with a student one-on-one about some aspect of their behavior, it works better to avoid talking about "what they did," but rather discuss a "pattern" of choices. Students seem less likely to challenge you when you are talking about a *range of behavior* than a *specific incident*:

Teacher: *Thanks for staying behind, Molly. I wanted to talk to you about a pattern of behavior.*

Molly: *I was just mucking around today with Phoebe. I wasn't really putting her down.*

Teacher: *I'm not talking about any one incident—I'm talking about a pattern of behavior.*

In video coaching, teachers will sometimes identify "sliding door" moments: the moment early in an encounter when the right phrase or word could have changed the outcome of their discussion with an argumentative student. "It's so obvious: why couldn't I see that at the time?" is the common refrain. Having quick ways to reframe discussions at your fingertips makes it more likely you will avoid unnecessary arguments and make the most of these "sliding door" moments.

Partial agreement

Another effective way to pivot around one of your student's arguments is to partially agree with what they are saying:

Resistance: *I wasn't calling out!*

Pivot: *Maybe you weren't, but I'll need you to listen carefully now to what Bethany is saying.*

Resistance: *It wasn't me who was doing it!*

Pivot: *Perhaps not. But everyone has now heard what my expectations are. Follow them, thank you.*

This approach works because instead of dwelling on who is right or wrong, the teacher pivots straight to what the student is expected to do from here on.

This can feel counterintuitive: It is hard not to be drawn in by the need to counter your students' arguments. It is for this reason that Tom Sherrington (2013), describing Bill Rogers' use of this strategy, refers to it as "being the Grown-up" as it "means teachers not trying to have the last word, or asserting their power in a situation when a student disputes their judgment."

The trade-off is that using partial agreement can stop you from falling into a common pattern: When people break rules, they tend to be defensive. They seek to legitimize their own perspective, and assert their "individual, private integrity" (Kegan & Lahey, 2012, loc. 1122). By partially agreeing with the student you subvert this pattern, leaving your student less defensive (they have nothing to argue with), and more open to suggestion. Partial agreement is a quick way to defuse a potentially tense encounter.

Acknowledging

Not all pivots involve pivoting around your student's argument. Sometimes you have to first acknowledge the emotion that is driving that argument. Many students come to school with a great deal of emotional baggage from fractured home lives or experience of trauma, and just getting to school is a major achievement. That they might be emotionally vulnerable and prone to being upset or angry is completely understandable. Similarly, students without the ability to self-regulate their emotions (those with mental health issues or executive function disorders, for example) or who are experiencing intense anxiety might find a classroom an incredibly stressful environment. It's not surprising that these students might sometimes react inappropriately.

Dealing with the challenges of helping these students is complex and time-consuming, and obviously not something you could possibly hope to address in a single exchange. But getting into the habit of empathizing with the student's emotional situation is something that can, over time, be useful in these situations. Our tendency as teachers is to reassure upset students or to offer them solutions to their problems. This can make students feel like we are failing to recognize their feelings or dismissing the significance of their problems. We need to take a moment to acknowledge these intense feelings.

My favorite way to do this is to use an "open response" (Mackay, 2006). This is a simple statement that characterizes your impression of the student's emotional state:

You seem frustrated . . .
You look upset . . .
You sound annoyed . . .
You seem out of sorts . . .

The ellipsis at the end of these statements is deliberate, as you are trying to create an opportunity for them to express how they feel—not adding advice about how to act in response to these feelings. "Do not give suggestions or instructions, or offer solutions. The solutions need to come from them," advises Mackay (2006, p. 70). If these solutions do come, it will be after the student has vented how they feel and returned to a state where they can really reflect, instead of wanting to fight or flee. Give them the space to do this.

When I coach teachers to use this strategy, their main concern is that they might misdiagnose the situation. "What if I ask them about being angry and they say they're not?" asked one teacher. "Won't that make them angrier?" Asking the wrong open prompt is common, but it still gives the student the chance to tell you what is the actual issue. Just treat the exchange as a chance to hear what feelings are driving their behavior, and accept that the student might not be able to articulate them but at least you have provided them with a moment of reflection.

We take a similar approach when we use a "mistaken goal" prompt (Lewis, 2012). In this approach you seek to diagnose the motivations of the student's off-task behavior back to them, in the form of a question (or a statement with rising inflection, which comes off as softer and gives the student less opportunity to contest the statement before it's finished):

It seems like you don't like being told what to do and just want to be in charge of yourself?

Did you really just need some extra attention?

Perhaps they made you feel bad and you wanted them to feel the same?

It felt like you didn't even try to take part because you didn't want to do it badly?

There is "a great risk of error" in these diagnoses, but again we are just trying to create an opportunity for students to think about what is driving their actions (Lewis, 2012, p. 105). Some feelings are so intense that they cloud judgment—this is as true for adults as it is for young people. Giving students a way to see more clearly what is motivating them helps them better understand their own emotions. Moreover, it helps them see that the way they are expressing their emotions is actually undermining what they want to happen. From this point, you can pivot the discussion to other, less problematic ways to meet their goals.

Sometimes registering how a student is feeling—and by extension why they are acting the way they are—is much simpler than this. Faced with an upset, angry, or withdrawn student, a simple acknowledgment in a supportive tone can go a long way to defuse a situation. I often see elementary or primary school teachers respond to all kinds of emotional behaviors with an earnest expression and a warm "OK." On paper, these exchanges don't look like very sophisticated teaching:

Student: *Then everyone else was saying my cat is short but she has really long legs!*

Teacher: *OK.*

However, if you saw this exchange on video you would understand the complexity of what has gone on here. The student, who has an explosive temper, seems on the edge of lashing out wildly at her tablemates. However, her face softens when her teacher, brow furrowed with concern, acknowledges her student's feelings with earnest OK, drawing out the word as she nods her head thoughtfully.

In middle or high school, you might achieve the same result with an acknowledgment pivot such as: "Well, that may be so . . ." My animated classroom behavior series *Toon Teach* (Campbell, Kenway, & Pearsall, 2017)—which was based on real classroom encounters—features an exchange that perfectly captures this pivot in action:

Reminder: *Can you sit down, Maddie?*

Response: *This is ridiculous. I've been to the counselor, I had to speak with Mrs. K., my mom's in the hospital, and now you're hassling me about this bull!*

Pivot: *Well that may be so, and I'm more than happy to talk about any of it, but can you just sit down first as I asked? Thank you.*

This is such a good example of acknowledging the student's emotions because the teacher doesn't react to the manifestation of that emotion ("bull") but hears what is driving it ("my mom's in the hospital") and offers the student a chance to talk about it. The fact that "Well that may be so" can also be used as a statement of partial agreement makes it a versatile phrase and one that you should keep in mind when you are building up your bank of potential pivots.

Things to remember

Sometimes a nonverbal response is a better option. Some students love to get teachers off topic. In fact, it is quite a common tactic for students who are being asked to get back to their work to distract with an irrelevant query. New teachers, for example, are often asked "How old are you?" or "Are you married?" Rather than even respond with a "That's not the issue right now," sometimes it is tactically better to ignore this altogether. If the student persists, raise your hand and signal with an open palm gesture that you are not engaging. You can then drop your arm but keep your palm opened in their direction as the signal not to interrupt further as you move on to engage other students. Finding the lowest level intervention that works is the key to dealing with off-task behavior (See Shift One: Low-Key Interventions). It is worth keeping in mind when you are about to use a pivot: Would a nonverbal intervention work just as well?

Finish with a directive. Redirecting, Reframing, and Partially Agreeing all end with the student being given a further direction to follow. The language you choose here is important. I often see teachers asking students to comply with this instruction:

Could you please get back to work?
Could you put your phone away and start the exercise please?

In most cases, these instructions work better as statements than questions. The issue is not up for further debate. Turning these questions into clear directives pivots the student straight back to their learning:

Get back to work, thanks.
Phone away and start the exercise, thank you.

Note that in each of these cases the teacher uses "thank you" rather than "please." "Please" can come off as a request for students to consider—or worse, as pleading—whereas "thank you" implies compliance. "Thank you" also acts as a punctuation point to your encounter, giving you a way to close the discussion with a firm directive.

Trial the phrases. The real strength of using a pivot phrase is that in the middle of a high-stakes encounter with a student you don't have to find the right words—you already have a range of carefully crafted phrases you can employ. You don't, in Paul Dix's (2017) words, have to "freestyle": "You don't need to improvise. The script is set," and this helps you avoid the trap of a "gradual crescendo of improvised castigation" (p. 93).

Keeping this in mind, try to stick to the language of the specific pivot you are trialing as closely as you can. You want to test whether that particular wording is effective and changing the language around makes this hard to do. I once had a video coaching session with a teacher who had been trialing "that's not the issue right now" as a pivot. He had decided that it "just doesn't work with my class" but when we watched the video, what he actually used was "that's just not the right issue," which is a different phrase altogether.

While showing fidelity to the phrasing of the pivot you've chosen is important, it is also important to trial different phrases. Look at this list:

That's not the issue right now . . .

Nevertheless . . .

I'm not talking about who you are—I'm talking about what you are choosing to do . . .

I am fair to everyone, but I don't treat you identically because you are not identical.

I'm not talking about any one incident—I'm talking about a pattern of behavior.

Maybe you weren't but I'll need you to . . .

Perhaps not. But now everyone has heard what my expectations are . . .

You seem frustrated . . .

You look upset . . .

You sound annoyed . . .

You seem out of sorts . . .

OK . . .

Well that may be so . . .

Be that as it may . . .

None of these will work for every teacher or in every situation. What you need to do is test as many different phrases as you can. Sometimes phrases work much better than you anticipate, so make sure you use them in real classroom situations to find out what is effective in your setting. Find the ones that suit your style of teaching and the kids you teach, and this way you'll have a wide range of potential options when one of your students is being resistant or argumentative.

Alternatives to pivot phrases

When I introduce pivot phrases in schools, I'm always asked, "What if they don't work?" This is understandable. As teachers, we are acutely aware of the limits of the strategies we use to address challenging behavior: Nothing works every time.

The short answer to this question is that we just move to a higher level of intervention. Typically, this is where the school's behavioral framework is implemented, with the teacher going through the more formal steps associated with a school-level response to serious off-task behavior. However, there are a couple of strategies you might try before you move on to these more serious modes of intervention.

Face-saving

As a new teacher, I tended to treat every off-task behavior as a considered action. I thought the student *chose* to behave badly and therefore my only possible response was to put in place serious consequences that reflected the deliberate nature of this behavior. Of course, this was unfair because a lot of these choices were actually incredibly impulsive. They were snap decisions and knee-jerk responses that the student would never have made if they had thought their actions through.

You need ways to allow your students to back away from their own poor choices. This might be something as simple as tactically ignoring a comment that is inappropriate. Or walking away from a student after you give them a directive—giving them time to complain about you or momentarily delay their compliance to show their friends that they aren't intimidated by your authority.

My favorite way to let students back away from bad choices is to use a face-saving statement. Essentially, these are just prompts that give students a chance to replay what they just said or did. They are a versatile strategy that you can use for different levels of off-task behavior. You can use these for low-level situations where the student spoke disrespectfully or used inappropriate language:

> **Student:** *This is such crap—Mr. L. is being a jerk.*
> **Teacher:** *Do you want to try that again?*
> **Student:** *Mr. L. won't let us out of class early to finish our photography project.*

Or you can use them as a face-saving "out" for a student who has lost their temper and has boxed themselves into a corner:

Student (screaming): *I am not going to do it and there's nothing you can do about it!*

Teacher: *I am going to walk away and let you calm down. Once you have, we will try this discussion again.*

Face-saving statements won't work every time any more than pivots will (I once asked a student "Can you replay that again with a quieter voice?" to which he replied with a shouted "No!"), but preparing some face-saving statements gives you some options for defusing potentially volatile situations. Here are some examples that I have used or seen used successfully in class:

Do you want to try that again?

I'll let you reconsider that choice . . .

Did you mean for that to happen?

Do you want to replay that?

Even a cursory study of the recent research on decision making (Kahneman, 2011) tells us that humans don't always make choices in a conscious and considered fashion. Face-saving statements give you another way to deal with young learners that acknowledges this fact.

Directed choice

In this strategy, you present a student with two options for resolving an issue and let them decide which course of action to take:

Teacher: *Put that away, thank you.*

Student: *No. It's mine—you can't tell me what to do!*

Teacher: *Either pop it in your bag or back in your pocket—you choose. Thank you.*

Typically, you use this strategy when one of your students is reluctant to comply with an instruction or being outright defiant. Rather than drawing on more of your authority to force the student to comply ("I said put it away! Now!"), you are offering them an opportunity to choose how to act. A directed choice gives students a greater sense of autonomy as they are being asked to extricate themselves from the dispute (Rogers, 2015).

Autonomy is a powerful form of motivation (Pink, 2009). This is especially true for young people—notice how many products marketed at young people offer the opportunity for customization. However, for this technique to be effective you have to offer students a genuine choice. Too often I see so-called directed choices being offered to kids where one of the choices being offered is completely unpalatable:

Put your phone away, Dante, or go to the assistant principal's office. You decide!

This is not a directed choice—it is a threat. Now, to be clear here, I have no problem with "when/then consequences." (Every student I have ever taught knows that if they use a racial epithet they will be immediately exited from the classroom.) For a directed choice, though, you have to present students with *two* choices that are likely to be acceptable to them:

Either put your phone back in your locker or in your bag, thanks.

You also have to give them the space and time to make their choice. I tell teachers that I am training in this technique that it is actually immediately before you implement it (when you are trying to formulate two legitimate choices as you approach the student) and immediately after you use it (when you are signaling them that the choice is really up to the student) that determine whether or not a directed choice will work. There a few simple steps to keep in mind here:

Make sure you move away quickly from the encounter (avoid the nervous glance back that telegraphs you are worried that they will comply) and engage another student about what they are working on. Make sure you are a fair distance from the misbehaving student and ideally at an angle that allows you to use your peripheral vision to assess whether there any signs the student is selecting one of the options you gave them.

Be patient. Give your student time to make up their mind. This is particularly important if the student is defiant, angry, or upset: You will need to wait long enough for both their audience (their table group, your whole class) to lose interest in the encounter (it is easier to back down when you are not playing to the crowd/for peer approval) and to calm down from their heightened emotional state.

After some time has elapsed, check in with the student in a low-key way. This might mean casting a silent eye on their progress as you circulate past their desk, or having a quick check-in with all of the students who are sitting in their area ("How are we going here, guys?"). Again, be patient. Try this approach two or three times—it will often take a student a while to take up the directed choice. If I see the student hasn't taken up the choice after a couple of check-ins I will use a micro script:

Have you decided yet or do you need more time?

I like this phrase because it is really just another directed choice, reiterating that it is up to the student to decide.

If the student doesn't take up this choice then you will have to resort to more formal processes. Make sure that when you do, you still emphasize that this is ultimately their decision. They have "decided" not to make a choice and the consequence of this is that they are "choosing" or "electing" to be involved in a formal process with potentially more serious consequences.

A directed choice isn't always taken up by the student, but it is a strategy well worth trying before you initiate more time-intensive interventions.

Micro-data tool—tracking pivots

Pivot phrases and other techniques for redirecting or reframing resistant behavior generally target individual students. As a result, you may use them only a few times in a lesson. Counting the total number of pivots isn't necessarily the best micro-data point; would using them more or less be a sign of success? It is better to track the *effect* of using pivots.

Teacher Movement Map: One technique I like to use when I'm coaching is to record the teacher movement as micro-data. Using a sketched map of the classroom, a peer observer or instructional coach traces your path around the class on the map with a gray lead pencil. This is a quick way to get a good sense of how you distribute your attention during a lesson. Those areas where you spend a lot of time become thick with entangled lines (some observers exacerbate this effect by going around and around a point if you linger there) while other areas of the class barely have any markings. If a particular student or group of students is monopolizing your time with argumentative behavior or the need for repeated interventions, this will be mapped out very clearly by this approach. This can be a striking visual benchmark against which to practice giving short, sharp commands and extricating yourself from unnecessary arguments with pivot phrases.

Interaction Timing: A similar approach is to time the amount of class time taken up by specific students. If a particular student often argues back, have an observer use a smartphone timer to record how much total time is taken up addressing their behavior. (This also works well if you take the data yourself but remember to hit "start" as you approach the student, as it is easy to forget to do this once an exchange has begun.) In my experience, just knowing you are being timed in these encounters is often enough to shift your behavior.

Being aware of the clock is an ongoing reminder to avoid becoming ensnared in debates and heightens your vigilance in looking for pivot points where you can redirect or conclude a conversation. That the metric here is a concrete number makes it easy to compare your efforts as you develop your skills at pivoting around or redirecting student resistance.

When I introduce this to teachers, I always mention an exchange I had with a middle school educator about this micro-data point approach. I had suggested trying interaction timing because he constantly found himself arguing with a particular student. After he had trialed the approach for a week, I asked him if the arguing had stopped: "No, she is as argumentative as ever—it's just that now I'm not around to hear it." Interaction timing is a useful micro-data measure because it helps you concentrate on the person over whom you have the most control: yourself.

Other tools: Aside from the two approaches discussed above you may wish to draw on other micro-data tools featured in this resource. Both the Affirmations vs. Commands Chart (Shift One: Low-Key Interventions) and the Verbal vs. Nonverbal Intervention Tally (Shift Three: Instructional Clarity) are good to use when addressing challenging behavior. Would it be better, for instance, to use a nonverbal intervention than a pivot in some situations? Would a specific student be less likely to resist if you gave them more contingent praise? Is it possible that when dealing with more extreme behaviors, you might have used some low-key intervention strategies less than you normally would have done—especially with the students whose behavior might have been overshadowed by these more extreme behaviors?

The *breadth* of different ways to measure the effect of pivoting and reframing behavior is important. Many of the issues that require you to use the strategies featured in this chapter are complex and hard to resolve. Being able to try different approaches and employ different micro-data tools helps you maintain a positive and proactive approach to these issues.

Summing up

Whether you are using these techniques to quickly pivot around half-hearted student dissent or using them to deal with more challenging behavior, your mindset is crucial here. When you first implement these techniques, you should view your attempts as a series of trials. It takes time to hone the subtleties of pivoting and reframing, and running a series of little experiments helps you remember that this is very much a matter of trial and error. This attitude is particularly appropriate if you are trying to address entrenched problems: It will help you persist for longer in the search for solutions to entrenched behavior and encourage you to view the inevitable moments when some of these strategies don't work with some professional distance.

This experimental mindset can be very empowering—many teachers who trial pivoting and reframing find that it gives them a greater sense of agency. Analyzing whether this or that mini-script works helps you focus not on the student's behavior but what you can do about it. A class where students exhibit challenging behaviors becomes something not to passively endure, but a chance to test new strategies. Selecting, testing, and refining the precise wording of a pivot phrase, for example, calls for subtle adjustments of your technique. Making small changes like these conveys a powerful message: The little things I do matter. This is something all teachers need to be reminded of sometimes.

When you start to use these techniques, take some time to identify what *types* of behavior you are seeking to change. Remember that the goal here is not relitigating specific arguments but rather trying to see the *patterns* of student resistance that you want to be able to address. The next step is to plan a response to these types of resistance. The advice from the conclusion to the last chapter applies here: Once you know what the routine patterns you want to change are, spot the cues that initiate these patterns and plan ahead for what routine you will replace them with. Be specific about precisely what you will do differently:

> *When Flynn starts calling out that the class is boring, I am not going to argue that it isn't, but rather remind him when the appropriate time for feedback is and insist that he complete the task.*

When the class is over, review the success of this intention.

Lastly, being aware of your own emotional state is important here. It takes time to get the wording, tone, and delivery of these strategies right but sometimes the real challenge of pivoting and recasting is negotiating the heightened emotional situations in which they need to be used. Getting angry or frustrated can undermine a pivot phrase more quickly than using the wrong wording. If a student is upsetting other students or being aggressive towards you it is understandable that you might have a strong emotional reaction but remember that there is a difference between this reaction and your subsequent professional response. Focus not on the behavior that has generated this response in you, but on the way you want the situation resolved. "In a potential collision," goes the analogy, "you don't look at the car coming at you but the gap in the road you need to steer toward."

Treating your adoption of these techniques as an experiment is a powerful way to put these strategies in action. It is not about being dispassionate or uncaring, but rather taking a *strategic* approach to helping students at their most combative and vulnerable—when they need your professional skills the most. Indeed, pivoting and recasting are techniques that allow you to steer around unhelpful behaviors and ultimately help students move toward the best version of themselves.

Shift Three: Instructional Clarity

Securing complete student attention before issuing instructions or making transitions

There are lots of moments in a class where you need your students to carefully listen to instruction, particularly as you introduce the lesson or move students between learning activities. Having techniques to ensure that you have your students' undivided attention and that they closely follow instruction is a key skill for effectively managing a class. If you find it hard to establish instructional clarity, it can undermine what you are teaching and make it difficult for your students to work out exactly what it is they are meant to do. Moreover, you can also waste a lot of your instructional time dealing with slow transitions between activities and off-task behavior.

Mastering the skills associated with getting your students' undivided attention and organizing their activities is a part of teaching that is often overlooked. While some classroom management theorists put an emphasis on developing these techniques (Lemov, 2015; Dix, 2017), I very rarely meet teachers whose college courses included instruction on establishing instructional clarity or specific training on how to move students from one activity to the next.

The "invisible" nature of this skill sometimes means that it is hard to identify precisely what is required of teachers here, which may be one reason why it appears to be inadequately taught. I have worked with many preservice teachers who felt unfairly critiqued by their supervisor after seemingly following their advice on lesson planning to the letter:

> *I did exactly what my supervisor told me to do and then she started adding all this extra stuff I should have done to make my lesson work. If she wanted me to do those things she should have mentioned them beforehand.*

In all likelihood, the supervisor was unaware of these teaching nuances until they were missing, and only then could she make explicit the techniques that she used without thinking.

We call this unconscious mastery "automaticity." Establishing instructional clarity is one area of teaching, in my experience, where teachers display a lot of intuitive skill, so it is important to analyze what goes into mastering this skill.

The Simple Shift here is the ability to effectively use a rallying call; from this one technique flows a cascade of other potential strategies. Once you can use this effectively to get your class's attention then you can employ a range of other strategies for making the most of that attention.

Rallying calls

Not letting your students talk over you is a golden rule of teaching. If you allow some of your students to chat during instruction, then it quickly becomes the norm for the whole class. Therefore, having a method for getting your students to focus and listen quietly to instructions is a crucial component of establishing instructional clarity.

Many teachers fall into the trap of trying to do this using volume and charisma. The problem is that, over time, this approach can become less and less effective (if it even worked in the first place.) As any parent knows, using a loud voice to get kids' attention is an exercise in diminishing returns. As students become habituated to your yelling, your current volume starts to lose its attention-holding authority and you find yourself having to be progressively louder to catch their interest. I often observe teachers whose "OK, let's get started" volume is the same as their "Stop, that's on fire!" volume.

You experience a similar attenuation of effect when relying on your personal charisma to garner students' attention. One of the key problems with the charismatic teacher model is that it relies on the teacher generating all the engagement with the learning. Students tend to be positioned as passive receivers of the lesson. ("I feel like they treat me like I am television," one teacher told me, "and they turn up and ask, 'What's on today?'") If you become too familiar to them, if some students don't make a personal connection to your teaching style, or even if you are just not "entertaining" enough, then very quickly kids can switch off.

When I coach teachers on instructional clarity, we often talk about how hard it is to *win* these situations. That is, it's hard for you to always have to personally demand and get your students' attention. It is easier to use routines to do the heavy lifting for you. Or to employ the analogy I often use in these coaching sessions: "Getting the attention of a raucous class is a bit like removing a stuck lid from a jar—sometimes it is easier to twist the jar rather than the lid."

The classic routine to use when you want the attention of your kids is a rallying call—a signal that your students need to quiet down and direct their attention toward you. There are many highly effective rallying calls, so the key is picking the one that suits your context. Obviously which one you employ will vary according to the space you work in, the age of your pupils, and the specific situation at that moment in your classroom, but the following rallying calls are effective examples of this technique.

Nonverbal signals

Sometimes, it is easier to show your students that you need their attention than it is to ask for it. A hand signal or gesture is a low-key way to get your class to quiet down and focus on you.

With an older class, you might simply raise your hand and wait for each student to stop speaking and do the same. Hands-up works well because of the subtle social pressure involved—note how when a student raises their hand they tend to then look at a student who hasn't done this yet. Or how when you use hands-up multiple times throughout a lesson, the last student to comply the previous time you used it is often one of the first the next time. It also gives clear signals about who has heard your request: The students who have raised their hands but are still chatting, for instance, aren't distracted—they are actively disobeying you and you can address this behavior accordingly.

With younger students, you can take a more "Simon Says" style approach, where you ask students to mirror your movements. I often work at an elementary school where the teachers of junior classes routinely punctuate their lessons in this way. For example, if a class of five-year-olds is unsettled during mat time, their teacher will simply mime a series of gestures (hands on heads, hands on shoulders, hands on heads again, and then hands in their lap) and the students will copy them. Once the students are focused on the teacher, she will pivot the students back to the task at hand.

Of course, hand gestures and other body-language cues aren't the only nonverbal rallying calls that teachers use. Many educators use devices such as whistles, bells, and alarms to get their students' attention. These devices allow you to cut through the noise of a classroom—or gymnasium, playing field, or workshop—without having to raise your voice. A good friend of mine who taught design technology (a shop class in the Australian state of New South Wales) would use the first lesson of the semester to get his students to rig up a doorbell and flashing light in his room. Thereafter, if he wanted to get his class's attention, he would just press the bell without ever having to shout above the din made by the machines in his workshop.

Moreover, sometimes using a noisemaking device allows you to subtly *externalize* yourself from this interaction. That is, you are not having to personally "win" your students' attention. For example, when your end-of-activity timer goes off, your students have to stop not because you have asked them to but because "that's the alarm." One of my favorite examples of this was a teacher at my sons' school who had a key chain sensor that would beep at loud noises. The key chain was designed so that if you lost your keys you could whistle loudly, and it would respond. However, she put it on a hook in her room and whenever a student yelled or the class got too rowdy, she would request the students to quiet down by noting: "OK guys, the key chain is telling us that we are too loud."

The power of all of these nonverbal rallying calls is that you can use them while expending little energy. For instance, compare the teacher who screams at the top of his lungs and gets no response from his students versus the teacher who employs a nonverbal signal and gets no traction with the class. The first teacher is liable to feel like his authority has been compromised, whereas the second teacher can simply move on to a marginally more intensive intervention. If your students don't respond to your nonverbal rallying call, you just move on to one of the countdown or call-and-response techniques described below.

Countdowns

Using a countdown ("5, 4, 3, 2, 1" or "1, 2, 3, look at me") is another popular way to get your students' attention. A countdown acknowledges that it takes some time to get an entire class of students to quiet down, and it gives students an opportunity to finish their thought, complete a sentence, or look up from what they are doing. Students won't always give you their attention instantly (this is reasonable; aren't teachers sometimes the same at staff meetings?) and using this type of rallying call allows for this delay. Indeed, when students are sluggish to respond to your rallying call, a countdown provides "cover"—if students are reluctant to comply, you simply slow down your count, maintaining your sense of authority while they slowly come around to following your instruction.

One of my favorite rallying calls is Waterfall. You simply count down "3, 2, 1, waterfall" and your students reply: "Shhh." The sound of even some of the class "shooshing" like that cuts through the other noise in the room and quickly gets the class's attention. There are dozens of variations of countdowns, and which one you use will depend on the age of the students: "1, 2, 3 look at me" is often used with young elementary schoolchildren while "5, 4, 3, 2, 1" is commonly employed in high schools. It is worth having a countdown as they are a useful tool for securing your class's attention.

Call and response

Many teachers I work with also use call-and-response routines to get their students' attention. Clapping out a beat and expecting the class to echo this pattern back to you is a classic example of this type of rallying call. So are all the two-part call-and-response phrases that teachers use. Here are some popular examples:

Teacher	Students
Quiet on the set . . .	action!
Hocus pocus . . .	time to focus!
Feeeed . . .	back!
If you can't make a mistake . . .	you can't make anything!
From three?	Swishhh!
Stop . . .	collaborate and listen!
Hands on top . . .	everybody stop!
L.I.S. . . .	T.E.N.
Hands on knees . . .	everybody freeze.
The teacher listens . . .	the students learn!

Focus One, Focus Two: Many of these call-and-response phrases are used almost exclusively in elementary schools. One of my favorite rallying calls is the Focus One, Focus Two technique which I have seen used successfully with students of all ages. How do you employ this technique?

If your class is working collaboratively and you want their attention, the first thing you do is to call out "Focus one." The students should then clap in unison as a response. Of course, a group of middle schoolers is not usually very good at immediately clapping back to you in unison. You will get a mix of off-beat claps while other students don't respond at all. Similarly, when using this technique with older students, you may get a smattering of desultory claps with students wary of responding too earnestly. That is OK: This technique is designed to anticipate this response. At this moment you simply repeat "Focus one." The second time you use this phrase you will get more students clapping, and doing so in a "tighter" fashion.

However, you still won't have everybody. So, the third time you call out "Focus two" and the students have to clap twice. The cadence of clapping twice is easier to do all together than clapping once—if you are behind the beat on the first clap, for example, you can catch up by clapping quicker on the second beat—and you will usually get a crisp transition into your next instruction.

Making rallying calls routine

As with all habits, being aware of the subtleties of how you implement your rallying calls will make it easier for using them to become part of an everyday routine. Following are some things to keep in mind.

Employ a bridging strategy

Just because you use a rallying call doesn't mean that every student will comply. In fact, you should *presume* that at first not everyone will respond to the call, and plan accordingly. What you need here is a bridging strategy—a technique to transition from the rallying call, through the moment when not all students are paying attention, to when they are carefully listening.

I think the simplest and easiest thing to do is get in the habit of thanking those who have complied and noting how many have yet to do so. (We note *how many*, rather than naming specific kids, because that way we address students who might be off-task but we haven't noticed.) This approach is often used in questioning ("I can see three hands up but I want more") where it is called "narrating" (Lemov, 2015), but I have found it works very well in this context. The key is that rather than giving a running commentary on who hasn't "obeyed," you keep the focus positive:

> *Thanks guys, that's good, I'm just waiting for three pairs of eyes. We're really starting to get this. Already, all but two of you are ready to hear my instruction. Much faster than yesterday, just waiting on one set of eyes now . . . Thanks, everyone, that was a fast transition.*

This acknowledges the students who are doing the right thing and nudges those who aren't to complete the routine without giving them specific attention. It is a simple strategy for addressing those in your class who aren't responding to your rallying call.

Use counter calls

Rallying calls can wear out: If you use the same rallying call again and again, it can become less effective. Your class may respond enthusiastically to the novelty of a new rallying call ("Everybody freeze!") but as it becomes more familiar, respond with only a desultory murmur. However, you don't want to have to come up with a brand-new rallying call every time you want your students to listen to you—the whole point of rallying calls is that they are a *routine*.

The easiest way to address this is to use a counter call. That is, every fourth or fifth time you ask for your students' attention, employ a second call as an alternative. For example, I regularly employ Waterfall with middle school classes but one in five times I will use Focus One, Focus Two for contrast. When instituting a rallying call with your class, make sure you identify an alternative call to keep the routine engaging when you want your students' undivided attention.

Do more with less

Another key to using a rallying call is to try to gradually reduce the intensity with which you deliver it. The first lesson you use "hands up," for example, you might wave your raised hand above your head and move around the room to make sure everyone has seen the signal. As the term wears on, though, you might just quietly raise a hand to around eye height while standing still. Similarly, a countdown might start as a high-volume count that gets a little quieter as your students progressively pay attention. However, once this is a familiar strategy, you can start at a much lower volume and then finish with just a silent count on your fingers.

Making your rallying calls gradually become more low-key makes for smoother transitions and, as with all low-key interventions, gives you a wider and more graduated range of options if it doesn't work.

"Badge" them as being for an older audience

Sometimes students are reluctant to engage with a rallying call because they associate them with younger grades, and teachers can believe this too. Of course, rallying calls are often used in the adult world: Judges use gavels, NBA referees use whistles, and large committees are called to order. However, if you worry that your kids might not adopt a rallying call for this reason, try suggesting that the routine is one you use with older students or adults:

> *OK, Grade 6, I wanted to show you a new rallying call: It is normally used with middle-schoolers, but I think you guys are mature enough to use it.*
>
> *I take it that as Year 12s you are responsible enough to follow a routine that college students use . . .*

Badging a specific rallying call as one for older learners is a quick and effective way to get over this inflection point and establish a routine way of securing instructional clarity.

Transition scaffolds

If you have already mastered rallying calls or are looking for ways to enhance this skill, transition scaffolds might be another threshold habit to explore (Bennett & Smilanich, 1994). A transition scaffold is a routine sequence of instructions that you use when introducing students to a task or when you are moving them between activities. I like that it takes something that you do intuitively and lays it out as a series of concrete steps.

There are seven of these steps, though I find it easier to remember them if you group these into four phases:

A. **Use a rallying call.** Demand **attention** using the routine you have established for doing this in your class. (Teacher waits with a raised hand for the class to be completely quiet: "OK guys, thank you.")

B. **When, what, and who.** Nominate **when** students are going to move. ("In two minutes, I'm going to move you out of your chairs, but I don't want you to move until then.") State **what** it is they are about to do as part of the next exercise. ("We are going to be exploring a new process for working mathematically with the goal of being able to solve the problem that we talked about yesterday.") Explain **who** they are about to begin working with in the next activity. Do not allow the group to move yet. ("We will work in groups of three and I don't want you to move yet, but you'll be able to select your trio. OK, please wait for my clap before you move.")

C. **Move now.** Give the students the **move now signal.** (Teacher claps.)

D. **Monitor and review. Monitor** the transition using teacher proximity—seek out potential off-task behavior and stand in the immediate vicinity of off-task students to ensure a quick transition. (Teacher moves to the back of the room to stand near a group of boys not yet in groups.) Give specific and positively framed **feedback** about successful transition behavior. ("Thanks guys, that was a much faster transition today.")

The structuring of this scaffold embodies a lot of clear, practical thinking. Phase A reminds us of the point made throughout this chapter—we need students' undivided attention before starting any instruction. Transition must begin from an orderly starting point, but in the hubbub of a busy classroom our tendency is to rush or skip this step. Phase A reminds us to avoid this trap.

The sequencing of Phase B is insightful. I have observed many classes (including my own) in which the teacher introduces a task by saying "We will be working in pairs today." They then go on to explain the activity—only to be ignored by the students as they clamor to choose their peer partners. Starting with "when," adding the "what" and then the "who" is a more logical and effective sequence and a good habit to establish with your class.

I also like the importance placed on having a "move now" signal in Phase C. A crisp, clear transition from one activity to the next is a hallmark of the high-performing teachers that I coach. Being mindful of this step helps you avoid students drifting off to the next task while you are still giving instructions.

The two final steps of Phase D emphasize a key insight: If you want your students to be better at something, give them fast, formative feedback about their progress. Naming transitions, observing, and giving the class feedback about how well they perform them is a good way to raise their awareness of the impact transitions have on learning time and establish tighter transitions in your classroom.

There are, of course, many other transition routines that are advocated by class management experts. For example, Paul Dix (2017) cites an example of a school that uses "fantastic walking" to explicitly describe how students move between classes. Doug Lemov (2010) mentions teachers who rehearse the distribution of worksheets or handing back of student work to improve the efficiency of those common practices. There is a good deal of merit in prescribing how to make class procedures routine. Indeed, both of the authors mentioned above only use these examples to make the wider point that describing, modeling, and practicing the procedures we use in class helps classes to run more smoothly.

I would suggest, though, that a transition scaffold might be a better place to start refining how your class makes transitions. This is because they are a threshold skill—they are actually a precursor skill that will make you better at explaining and implementing these other routines. Focusing first on what you do—rather than what the kids do—is the key here. When you are adopting a new classroom habit, I think it is best to start with the element over which you have the most control: you.

Do now activities

As rallying calls and transition routines become more automatic, it is easier to establish routines that require very little teacher intervention at all. By way of conclusion I thought it might be useful to look at an emblematic example of this type of routine—a "do now" activity (also known as "bell ringer" activities).

"Do now" activities are a simple routine for beginning a class without the teacher having to immediately give students verbal instructions. They are useful because at the beginning of the class you have so many competing demands for your time: procedural requirements like taking attendance, students clamoring for help with their homework or providing reasons why they couldn't get it done, disputes from the playground to adjudicate, seating plans to enforce, the students who are in dire need of extra help or a moment of recognition, and then students who are tardy arriving just as everything else has been settled....

So what does the alternative to this look like?

Students enter the room where a short exercise that they have to complete is prominently displayed on the board. This short task should require little teacher direction, involve individual written work, and take around 3–5 minutes (Lemov, 2010).

Your students immediately start this task (do now). One of the biggest advantages of this approach is that even if students arrive in dribs and drabs the exercise can begin immediately. This is particularly effective for latecomers: Having the other students already quietly working is a powerful social cue about what is expected of them. Moreover, if you have to address this tardy behavior, you can do so without having to split your attention with the instructional needs of the group.

The "do now" task introduces the learning to come. For me, the key to this task is making sure the "do now" task is *not* busy work, but rather something explicitly linked to the rest of your lesson. Many teachers ask students to do 5–10 minutes of "free reading" as a way to settle the class, and while this can have its place, I think it is far more meaningful if the "do now" task introduces the student to the learning for that lesson. If you are about to have a class debate on the merits of genetic engineering, then asking students to "list five reasons parents either should or should not be able to decide the height and eye color of their children" would be an effective "do now." Or if you are doing a marine biology revision lesson on squids and cuttlefish, asking students "to write a paragraph to summarize the key features of cephalopods in exactly 21 words" is a great lesson starter.

Micro-data tools: Tracking instructional clarity

There are two distinct types of tools you can use to review how you are using instructional clarity: those that focus on student behavior and those that look at the steps you take to secure that instructional clarity as you move students between activities.

Attention Cues Tally: Of those aimed at students, I find that an Attention Cues Tally is a good place to start. (See micro-data tool on page 56). The person observing waits until you need to get your class's attention and then notes in the left column when you use verbal comments to get students to listen and in the right column when you use a nonverbal signal such as a hand gesture or proximity to get them to pay attention.

MICRO-DATA TOOL

Attention Cues Tally

Verbal interventions	Nonverbal interventions
Repeating your instruction, naming the student and directing them to comply, discussing the impact of the student with the student, etc.	Using hand signals, facial expressions, or your spacing in the room to cue the student to pay attention.
TOTAL:	**TOTAL:**

Attention Cues App: Alternatively, you might do this using an app. The one I use for teacher coaching is available on the McREL website, at mcrel.org/tiltingyourteaching. It presents the ratio of verbal to nonverbal reminders as an easy-to-digest, color-coded pie chart.

Whichever approach you take, remember that it is not the case that nonverbal interventions are good and verbal interventions are bad. Sometimes a sharp verbal interjection is essential: "Step away from the lathe—you aren't wearing your goggles!" Rather than assessing whether you are using the *correct* strategy, use this tool to heighten your awareness of the options open to you in securing your students' attention. A good way to do this is to ask yourself: "If I taught that lesson again, would I use the same ratio of nonverbal to verbal commands?" I have found in teacher coaching that this simple reflection question can go a long way to helping educators increase this awareness.

Consistent Corrections Chart: When you are aiming to become more aware of securing your students' attention, another useful data point is how consistently you address off-task behavior. When I observed classes, I used to do this for teachers by making a dash on a pad whenever I spotted a student doing the wrong thing, and then crossing through that mark if the behavior was then corrected by the teacher. Jim Knight (2018) has a more formal version of this tool called a Consistent Corrections Chart. This requires the observer to list common off-task behaviors, record when they occur and, in the column next to this, note whether the teacher addressed them.

Monitoring off-task corrections isn't easy to do "live"—it is hard to watch every student's actions all at once—so most teachers only use this tool for lessons recorded on video. But it is well-suited to taking data on rallying calls because they occur over a discrete period of time and the expectations on student behavior are narrowly defined. When you use a rallying call, ask your observer to record whenever a student doesn't follow your signal to stop what they are doing and give you their attention. They then note if you pick up on this or if you start your instruction without checking this behavior. Whether you choose to use a Consistent Corrections Chart to do this or just record corrections with hash marks and crossing out on a pad, this is a simple way to refine how you use rallying calls.

Making transitions

If you have already mastered getting your students' undivided attention, you might want to spend some time honing the transitions between activities in your classroom. Some subjects have a high number of transitions in the course of an average lesson. These can be time-consuming, disrupt the flow of the lesson, and increase the opportunities for off-task behavior. Bennett and Smilanich (1994) have written insightfully about the importance of effective transitions and the procedures required to implement them.

When you multiply the amount of time spent on transitions in your average lesson by lessons in a week and teaching weeks in a year, this can be a sobering figure. I have found that using micro-data tools as a "Fitbit-style" reminder is one of the quickest ways to reduce this number and maximize instructional time in your class.

Transition Timing: Many teachers start this process by timing transitions using a stopwatch on their smartphone, and then calculating how much of the lesson time is used transitioning between activities. This heightens their awareness of the transition time involved in an average lesson and provides a benchmark for minimizing this non-instructional time.

Transitions Scaffold Checklist: The transition scaffold template, as displayed below, is a quick checklist that helps you do this. You can use an observer to take this data or take it yourself on video. However, because it is so simple—you just have to put a dash or dot in the square when you complete a step in this sequence—many teachers find that they can take this data themselves as they are teaching.

Transitions Scaffold App: The app version of this scaffold, which is also available at mcrel.org/tiltingyourteaching, is equally easy to use and not only shows you when you have missed a step but when you have completed these steps out of sequence, which is a common error when first using this scaffold.

MICRO-DATA TOOL

Transitions Scaffold Checklist

Use a rallying call to demand *attention*.	State *when* students are going to move.	State *what* it is they are about to do.

If you are working on transitions for the first time—particularly if you are doing so without a peer partner or teacher-coach to take data for you—try concentrating on one phase of the transition at a time. Pick the phase of the transition you think you use the least and use the data tool as a cue to see if you can improve the consistency with which you use the techniques involved with this phase. My experience is that using this data tool a few times is often enough to embed this mini-habit. You can then concentrate on developing this level of consistency with the rest of the transition scaffold.

MICRO-DATA TOOL

Transitions Scaffold Checklist (*continued*)			
Explain *who* they will work with in the next activity.	Give the students the *move now* signal.	*Monitor* the transition using teacher proximity.	Give specific feedback about the transition.

Summing up

Establishing instructional clarity is about consistency. The techniques for getting your students to give you their undivided attention are not complex, nor are the skills associated with creating orderly transitioning routines in your classroom. What they do require is regular and consistent use so they become routine for you and your students. You want to use them enough that the moment you initiate a transition or employ a rallying call, your students will automatically know what to do—and do it quickly and quietly. And you need to be able to employ them when you're under stress—when the class is rowdy or you're pressed for time—because this is precisely when it is most important to demonstrate consistency.

Anticipate too that the take-up of these routines might be uneven. Some teachers might have instant success, but it is more likely that some students will respond to a rallying call while others treat it with studied indifference. If you have a noisy or distracted class, focus on the bright spots. The key to establishing a rallying call with a rowdy or resistant group is to "scale success." Try a variety of different rallying calls to see what works best with your group. Take careful note of who does comply with your instructions and make sure they get acknowledgments for being early adopters of this routine. A real trap with rally calls is to give negative feedback about failure to respond to the class as a whole group, frustrating those students who have actually complied with the instruction. Similarly, when giving the class feedback on slow transition times, make sure you present these times as a range, acknowledging those students who move from one activity to the next quickly. ("That took us a whole minute, guys, but the group in the corner did it in 25 seconds which is excellent—let's see if we can get it down to that.") When you have a core of students doing the right thing, then you can use proximity and other reminders to nudge the rest of your students to meet this standard.

The other thing to be aware of when you are establishing instructional clarity is your own presence—it is much easier to secure your students' undivided attention if your body language suggests authority. Take up a balanced stance in a position where most of your students can see you. (If you use the same position in the room to issue rallying calls, it can help cue students you are about to use this technique.) Then use crisp, clear gestures or calls to signal what your class has to do.

Avoid a hesitant tone or equivocal body language—act as though you expect everyone to comply and adopt a demeanor that reflects this. Don't rush this: Pausing for students to do what is asked of them is a big part of securing their undivided attention.

All this work for such a small component of a lesson might feel a little out of proportion, but the effort is worth it. Establishing instructional clarity is a Simple Shift because once we have our students' undivided attention, there is so much we can do with it.

Shift Four: Wait Time

Extending the amount of thinking time you give your students *before* expecting them to respond to questions

If you want your students to provide high-level responses, you need to give them enough thinking time to do it.

I once observed a teacher ask one of her students: "How does the entire history of Christianity inform this text?" The student was, understandably, dumbfounded, but after a moment you could see that they were trying to formulate an answer. Before they even got to offer a suggestion though, the teacher bounced the question to the person next to them: "How do *you* think it informs the text?"

When I showed the teacher the coaching video of the class she was appalled. I tried to reassure her that rushing was an easy habit to fall into—after all, as teachers we are just so busy and have such a challenging amount of curriculum to get through—but she cut me off: "*I* don't even know the answer to that question!"

When I tell teachers about this exchange they often laugh, not in judgment over a fellow teacher's mistake but in a moment of sharp recognition—they have fallen into this trap too. It's a common mistake: We have 50 years of evidence (Rowe, 1972; Tobin, 1987; Stahl, 1994; Marzano et al., 2010) to say that the time between when teachers ask a question and when they expect an answer is very short. Typically, teacher wait time averages around only a second (Cazden, 2001).

Wait time is a Simple Shift because extending your average wait time by a couple of seconds is not hard to do and can have such profound effect on your students' learning.

Let's look in more detail at the benefits of longer wait times.

More students offer answers. In many cases, only a small number of students routinely respond to questions put to the whole group (Black & Wiliam, 2014). These are typically students who think quickly and have confidence, whether in the subject matter or more broadly within their peer group, and narrowing the responses to this self-selecting group is problematic. For the benefit of all students, and for the quality of class discussion, we obviously want to encourage more students to answer questions and create a class culture where all kinds of thinking are validated.

Extending wait time is a remarkably easy way to do this. By establishing a habit of providing this regular "thinking space," we include students who need more processing time, or are initially hesitant. It also nudges those students who ordinarily give a reflexive "don't know" answer, and reminds them that you are interested in their current thinking, not some predetermined answer.

Longer wait time after questioning increases the number of students who will regularly answer questions, and the research bears this out (Marzano et al., 2010).

Student answers are more detailed and sophisticated. Extending wait time not only increases the number of your students who will answer questions but improves the quality of their answers. I often see this when I'm coaching: A teacher extends their wait time and their students almost immediately start producing longer and more considered responses. Obviously, it is easier to answer more thoughtfully with more thinking time and focusing on wait time helps ensure this is an everyday opportunity for students.

Students are more likely to speculate. In classes where the teacher asks rapid-fire questions, those who already know the answer tend to dominate. By contrast, in classes where teachers wait longer there is more room for conjecture. Giving your students more reflection time increases the number of students who hazard a guess or offer up their initial impressions (Rumhor,

2013). This benefit was identified in the earliest work on questioning (Rowe, 1972) but is an often overlooked advantage of extending wait time.

However, as with all the Simple Shifts, the biggest advantage of offering students more wait time is that it changes *your* mindset. This approach recasts your thinking in a couple of crucial ways that are closely related.

Teachers understand the need to make room for student voices. Teachers talk too much. They dominate classroom conversation, taking up, on average, 70 to 90 percent of available class time (Hattie, 2012). This creates a class culture in which students expect to be passive listeners, rather than active learners. Using extended wait times is a powerful reminder for us that what matters most is not what is being taught but what is being learned.

Teachers see questioning as a way to elicit feedback. In the busy environment of the classroom, it is easy for questioning to become a rote exercise where the teacher knows the answer and queries students till someone comes up with the "right" response. (I certainly have been guilty of playing this game of "Guess what I'm thinking.") Extending wait time reminds us that when we question our students we are actually asking "What are you thinking?" not "Who has the answer?" Having more of your students respond, in greater detail, with more thought and speculation, has a powerful flow-on effect: You get a better sense of what precisely is each student's point of need. Extending wait time improves the amount and quality of feedback you receive from students and makes it easier to work out where they most need help.

Reducing the dominance of the teacher's voice and eliciting more student feedback is a key characteristic of high performing teachers (Hattie, 2009). Expert teachers are constantly assessing the effect of their teaching:

- Did my students engage with the lesson?
- For whom were my methods useful?
- Who requires a different technique or more support?
- What changes can I make to maximize the effect of my instruction?

Indeed, Hattie and Zierer (2018) argue that this is the key "mind frame" of effective teaching: "Educational expertise is shown by how teachers think about what they do. One of the most crucial questions is whether teachers want to know about the impact" (p. 2).

When I coach other teachers, I have noticed that introducing or refining their use of wait time is one of the best ways to get them thinking about the impact of their teaching. As one teacher put it to me with a broad grin: "Who'd have thought making sure the kids were doing the thinking and not just me would make for better lessons?" This comment is telling because our coaching conversation was specifically about wait time but her comment made a wider point about feedback. Wait time is a classic example of a threshold habit because it opens teachers up to a cascade of other opportunities and strategies by changing your mindset.

I routinely see this in schools where I establish video coaching programs. If you have above-average wait time—as little as three seconds is enough (Marzano, 2017)—my experience says you will find it easier to "cold-call" students, ask inverted questions, unpack learning intentions, elicit responses from struggling students, provide verbal feedback, and foster peer-to-peer reflection.

Wait time strategies

If extended wait time is so beneficial why don't more teachers use it routinely? "Most teachers find increasing wait time difficult," observe Dylan Wiliam and Siobhan Leahy, "partially because changing any habitual practice is hard" (2015, p. 71). This is a helpful insight: Extending wait time is a simple change but that doesn't mean that it is easy. You have to avoid defaulting into old habits, especially when things are hectic or your workload is overwhelming. (When I made this point in a workshop, one participant dryly added: "You mean all the time?") However, there are a number of strategies you can use to make it easier to make extended wait times part of your teaching routines.

Here are some examples that I have found particularly useful for helping teachers with this Simple Shift.

Turn and talk

Using Turn and Talk with your class is the easiest way to improve your wait time. Rather than starting questioning by cold-calling individual students, you present the question to the whole class and let them discuss possible responses with a partner. This doesn't have to be very long to be effective. Between 45 and 90 seconds of Turn and Talk time is ample—indeed my video analyses of classes suggest that after this time you get diminishing returns as students start to talk about other topics. However, this still represents a significant amount of extra thinking time for your students.

Turn and Talk time is a shortened version of Think, Pair, Share, where students are asked to consider the question for 30 seconds or so of quiet reflection before discussing it with a partner. Both of these approaches work well and ensure that all of your students have the opportunity to be involved in a discussion about the question, rather than just the students you call on. When discussion time ends, use a rallying call (see Shift Three: Instructional Clarity) to get the class's undivided attention and then select a student to give their response. Language here is important. I find that instead of asking students for the answer, it is better to ask something like, "What did you and your partner talk about?"

This seems less intimidating and offers students a layer of protection: You are neither asking for *the* answer nor *their* answer but rather a summary of their discussion.

Similarly, some teachers find it useful to talk about "responses" rather than "answers" (Walsh & Sattes, 2016). Remember, the point of questioning is to find out what your students are thinking, and not just who knows the answer. Using qualifying language such as "might" or "could" can also work well to take the pressure off a student and encourage them to explain their thinking (Pearsall, 2018):

What was you and your partner's response to this question?

or

What did your group think the answer to this question might be?

It is easy to see why students might find these adjustments give them more confidence to respond.

Pre-cueing

You can also use pre-cueing to extend your wait time. Pre-cueing is just giving individual students advance notice of the question you are going to ask them:

Adrian, in five minutes, I'm going to ask you to define "representative democracy."

Students process information at different speeds (Pope, 2013). Pre-cueing questions allows you to differentiate wait times so students have all the time that they personally need to consider the question and formulate their response. For example, if a student has auditory processing problems they might struggle to formulate a response in the quick back-and-forth of a class discussion. However, if you give them a written version of the question you will pose a few minutes before the discussion starts, they can take a more active part in the class's conversation.

Another way to extend wait time is to use the so-called rolling cue. This is where you give advance notice to students about the order in which you will solicit answers:

> *I'm going to ask Keiran to explain the role of the Senate, then Kyle, and finally someone from the back-table group.*

This way the first student has a few seconds wait time, the second might have 30 seconds, and the last student a minute or more to consider their answer. As a teacher coach, I often observe that teachers who employ pre-cueing find it easier to extend their wait time—especially in mixed ability classrooms.

Be challenging *and* supportive

It is not enough, though, to give students time to think—we have to encourage them to use this time well. This requires a delicate balancing act: We want students to be supported so they are prepared to take risks, but we also want to challenge those students who don't contribute because of a lack of effort or attentiveness. The following are some strategies that help students make the most of their thinking time.

Legitimize speculation

Your students are more likely to engage with a question if they feel that they don't have to be "right" to contribute. For this reason, you might find it useful to talk about "responses" rather than "answers," as mentioned earlier (Walsh & Sattes, 2016). Many teachers in my video coaching programs, for example, find this small shift very effective for encouraging more student responses. One teacher I worked with succinctly summarized why this works so well: "It's a way of showing my kids that the point of questioning is to find out what they are thinking, not just who knows the answer . . . and reminding myself of this too!" Similarly, using qualifying terms such as "might" or "could" encourages more students to engage with the question. This is sometimes described as giving questions a "speculative frame" (Pearsall, 2018). Again, it is a minor change but even a quick comparative example (*OK guys: What's the answer?* versus *What does your group think the answer to this question might be?*) makes it easy to see why your students might find it easy to speculate when you subtly modify questions in this way.

Prompting

We can also encourage students to make the most of wait time by directing their thinking as they contemplate answering the question. For example, you can celebrate students who are prepared to offer answers as a way to encourage others to join in—an approach that is sometimes called "narrating hands" (Lemov, 2015). What does this sound like? In an elementary setting, something like this:

> *I can already see five risk-takers with their hands up! Who else is going to offer a response?*

Or you might prompt older students on how to think about their response:

> *I see students checking their notes to see how to do this.*
>
> *I'm interested in seeing if people can make links with yesterday's learning.*

Prompting takes some finesse: You want to offer some scaffolding but if you talk too much, you take away from the student's thinking time. One solution I have found useful is offering students some sentence starters on the board. It is easier to articulate an insight if the language demands of presenting this response are reduced (Olson, 2011). Giving your students sentence starters such as *I would like to challenge that idea* or *The evidence suggests that* provides them with the scaffolded language to help them formulate a response.

Cold calling

Cold calling is asking a question and then identifying a student to respond, as opposed to simply waiting for the most confident and able students to volunteer their answers.

> *Why does the author have this character do this? . . . Fiona?*

This approach ensures that students use their wait time properly as they are aware that the teacher might ask them for a response even if they don't have their hands up. Again, this takes some finesse. It is important that you explain to your students why you conduct class discussion this way. It is also important that you don't fall into the trap of using this approach to target students who aren't listening, lest students start to see cold calling as a form of punishment. One way to ensure students see this process as fair is to randomize who gets called on. Many teachers use a cup of Popsicle sticks labeled with students' names from which they can draw the next speaker (Wiliam, 2011), or you might try using one of the many apps that make random selections from a class list. Remember, though, to make your random selection after posing the question. Naming the question first tends to turn students into spectators:

What will Finley say to that?

Whereas posing the question first and then pausing provokes a very different response:

How would I answer that?

If you do cold-call, you should anticipate that more of your students will respond with a knee-jerk "I don't know." (Very young students often use "I forgot" in the same unthinking way.) Having a strategy for addressing this instant response means students are less likely to try to duck a question directed at them.

My favorite way to do this is to use the question relay technique (Pearsall, 2012), which sounds like this:

I don't know.

OK, you are not sure. (Or: OK, you don't know yet.) I'm going to ask two other students what the answer could be and then come back to you to see which of those you might have used in your answer.

This doesn't work every time (sometimes both of the other students you call on say "I don't know" too, which tells you the question might be too hard). However, it does send a clear signal that in your class "I don't know" is not the end of thinking but the start of it.

Managing other students

Any discussion of how to extend your wait time has to acknowledge that one difficulty you face when implementing this strategy is your students interrupting one another. It is hard to encourage a student to take their time and reflect on their response when another student just blurts out their response or starts mucking around. Teachers need strategies for dealing with off-task behaviors or those situations where a student's enthusiasm just gets the better of them.

Elsewhere in this book we explore strategies for dealing with off-task behaviors (see Shift One: Low-Key Interventions) and these interventions are particularly useful for dealing with students who are behaving inappropriately in class discussion. However, it is also worth addressing how to deal with students who call out, interrupt, or just want to answer every single question. These behaviors are expressions of engagement—they happen because the student wants to add to the class discussion—so we don't block these behaviors, we guide them. The following strategies are some effective methods for doing this.

Pause gesture

This is a quick nonverbal signal to indicate that the student just needs to hold their thought for a moment: for example, raising your arm to indicate that the student needs to put their hand up and wait, or reaching out toward the student with a raised palm as a "not yet" signal. The nuances matter here: If you raise your arm to suggest "hands up," you usually then turn a little away from the student to cue them that they don't have a license to just go on with what they are saying now that their hand is up, but still have to wait. Similarly, teachers who use a raised palm as a "not yet" signal find that it works best if they then drop their arm but keep their palm raised for a much longer period of time to ensure their students respond to this cue.

Talking tokens

This is a structured conversation activity where you give your students two tokens (sticky notes, raffle tickets, etc.) each, and every time they make a contribution to class discussion you take away one of their tokens. Once both of their tokens have been taken they have used up their opportunities to talk and need to give other students the chance to use all of their tokens before it is their turn again. By limiting the number of responses a student can give, this approach encourages able kids to focus on the quality rather than the quantity of their contributions to class discussion: They very quickly learn that they need to "ration" their answers and respond to only the most challenging questions.

This approach also encourages those students who are normally "crowded out" by the volume of answers from intellectually dominant classmates to find their voice. If you want to trial this strategy, it is worth noting that teachers who use talking tokens most effectively make it clear to students that a contribution is not just an answer, but it might also be a question, clarification, or just asking the teacher to re-explain what they are discussing.

One-on-one discussion

If neither of these approaches works with a student who is dominating class discussion, you can take them aside and make an arrangement for them to only answer more-challenging questions. This works best if you first acknowledge their successful contributions to class discussion ("You've answered those foundation questions so well, you don't have to answer them anymore!") and then explain that now you will be targeting them with more interesting and challenging questions. (I recently had this conversation with an elementary student who was delighted by this, citing a computer-game analogy: "Have I leveled up?" Clearly he understood that he had graduated to a new skill level in class discussion.)

I usually arrange a signal with the student (the phrase "follow up" is a versatile example) to help them ready themselves for when a higher-order question might be targeted at them.

Here is an example from a science class where the teacher was trying to extend a student I'll call Sam:

> *That's correct, Grayson, argon is an inert gas. As a follow up, can anyone explain to me why a nonreactive gas might be useful? Sam?*

This approach makes it possible to differentiate your questions to students of different abilities while running a whole-class discussion in which everyone has enough time to think.

Micro-data tool: Tracking wait time

It can be hard to assess how much wait time we actually offer our students. Even a short period of time after a question when your students aren't responding can feel like an eternity in a classroom. As a result, we often overestimate the length of wait time we use. Tracking this data is an important strategy for helping you embed a longer wait time in your teaching.

Wait Time Dot Chart: I have found that one of the most effective ways to record this information is to employ the micro-data tool below. To use it, the person taking the data simply notes when you ask a question and counts to three. When you interrupt your wait time in any fashion—call on a student to answer, bounce to someone else, change the question, or answer it yourself—they stop counting. If your wait time is less than three seconds the observer puts a dot or dash in the left-hand column. If it is three seconds or more they do the same in the right-hand column. A peer partner or instructional coach can take this data as a class observer but videotaping a short snippet of your students in class or small-group discussion and then taking the data yourself is also instructive.

MICRO-DATA TOOL	
Wait Time Dot Chart	
Wait time < 3 seconds	Wait time > 3 seconds
TOTAL:	TOTAL:

Alternatively, you can use an app to do this. The Wait Time app, available at mcrel.org/tiltingyourteaching, combines the tally chart above with a timer and provides you with a graph summarizing the ratio of wait times above and below three seconds as well as an average wait time figure. It is an intuitive and easy-to-use tool with which to hone the silences in your questioning.

Wait time is a fairly automatic practice and using an app to measure it can help you observe your use of wait time in a more self-conscious way. In small-group video coaching sessions, I often ask teachers: "If someone else had to take your lesson, what advice would you give them about wait time?" This both helps acknowledge the context in which the lesson is being taught—sometimes there are specific reasons why the wait time is necessarily low—and gives teachers a little distance from which to view their own practice. Try asking this question yourself when you are looking at your own wait time data.

Wait time effect: You might also want to measure the *effect* of using more wait time. One of the core benefits of wait time is that more students take an active part in the learning. You can note this using a class list. Simply put a tally mark next to each student who answers a question. By the end of the discussion you will have a rough record of class participation that you can use as a benchmark against which to measure your subsequent efforts to engage more students with extended wait times.

These tools aren't just effective for introducing extended wait time into your teaching, but for consolidating it. The first research on wait time showed that teachers tended to fall back into old habits after using it effectively for three or four weeks (Rowe, 1972)—something that reflects my experience as a teacher coach. However, reintroducing a micro-data tool a month or so into using this approach goes a long way to getting you past this inflection point.

Summing up

Wait time is usually an unconscious habit. It's not that we *decide* to wait only a second before we expect a student to answer; it's a habit we have developed over the course of our teaching. Indeed, it may not even be originally *our* habit. Our class routines develop not just from our experiences as teachers but what we go though as students: "Teachers have spent thousands of hours in classrooms as students, where they internalize the scripts of how classrooms operate" (Wiliam, 2016, pp. 185–186). This is why, Wiliam goes on, even novice teachers find it hard to depart from seemingly short-lived practices to take up more innovative approaches.

The micro-data tools above will help make you more aware of your unconscious practice. Sometimes teachers get a little disheartened when they take wait time data for the first time. Don't be worried—remember the research says most teachers have quite low wait times. Your first micro-data figure is just a benchmark against which to measure your improvement, which can happen quite quickly. Many of the teachers involved in small-group video coaching sessions I facilitate see positive results within two weeks.

However, this is not true of every teacher. My advice is to start small. You are setting yourself up for a fall if you go from having no extended wait time to immediately having very long wait times, because students need time to get used to this change of practice too. I usually advise teachers to tell their class about what they are doing and why they are changing their practice to facilitate this change. It contextualizes why a class routine they have come to view as the natural order of things is suddenly changing—and it is helpful that the occasional student will take real pleasure in giving you a "reminder" when your practice doesn't match your stated goals.

Proceeding slowly also feels less onerous. In *Mini Habits: Smaller Habits, Bigger Results* (2013), Stephen Guise has noted how focusing on tiny changes of action reduces internal resistance to adopting new habits. Trying to add one second to your wait time for one lesson doesn't feel like a daunting prospect, even in a busy working day, but it might be enough to encourage more students to answer your questions with more thoughtful responses. Moreover, if the goal is very small you are much less likely to feel the negative "feelings . . . that come with goal failure" (p. 19). If extending your wait time just a little doesn't work, it doesn't feel like a substantial failure or a revealing flaw in your teaching (or your character), but a mini-experiment that requires some tweaking.

This tweaking is worth the effort. Extending your wait time by as little as a second or two can have a substantial effect on the way you and your students view, use, and respond to questioning. As a change of practice that requires little preparation or additional workload (Pearsall, 2018), it is a classic example of a Simple Shift—a small change of habit that can have a profound impact on your students' learning.

Shift Five: Pause and Elaboration Time

Extending the length of time you pause *after* your students answer to encourage them to elaborate

If you want students to give detailed and thoughtful responses to your questions, you need to make sure you get to hear their extended thinking.

As a graduate teacher, I once watched a teacher run a group discussion with a class I taught and was surprised by how comprehensive the students' answers were in this master class session. What stood out was how she responded to my students' answers. My own tendency was to jump in immediately after one of the kids responded with an evaluation or encouragement: "That's right!" or "Nearly . . . good try" or "Yes, that's correct because . . ." Her approach was different: Instead of immediately evaluating the student's response, she just offered neutral statements that made space for further elaboration.

My students readily took up this opportunity to elaborate, self-correcting and adding detail to their answers. One student who had only ever answered my questions in the most cursory way offered her a detailed justification for his thinking. This really surprised me—it was like he was an entirely different student. I vividly remember wondering: "Have I truncated every answer my students have ever given me?"

If you routinely wait a second or so after a student answers a question, you can substantially improve the quality of your students' responses. We have looked at how extending wait time—the time you take after you ask a question—can have a substantial impact on the quality, frequency, and variety of student answers. In this chapter, we'll extend this same concept to the time *after* a student answers—what I refer to as Pause Time. In the United States it is often referred to as "wait time two," whereas in the United Kingdom it is more often labeled "elaboration time" (Wiliam & Leahy, 2015). Regardless of what terminology you're familiar with, the key idea here is that the "use of silence is critical to deep and productive discussion" (Walsh & Sattes, 2016, loc. 480).

Wait time and pause time are obviously similar, and it can be confusing to remember which is which. When we ask a question, we wait for a response, and when we get that response, we pause to allow students to refine and elaborate their thinking. And though the concept behind each is the same, the techniques for increasing pause and wait time are different.

Why is this Simple Shift so effective?

Students elaborate more frequently

Using pause time gives your students an opportunity to flesh out their response. In video coaching sessions, we see that extending pause time makes students more likely to justify their reasoning or offer supporting examples. This is particularly important in classroom discussions because they are "asymmetric"—students and teachers have very different levels of authority as to who can speak and when (Maroni et al., 2008)—and this means young people anticipate interruptions and tend to talk in short bursts (Hattie & Zierer, 2018). Students need a clear signal that they can discuss their thinking at length, and using pause time helps make this message clear.

Students clarify their thinking

Using pause time also helps students develop their answers. Many students won't contribute to class discussion because they "don't have the answer." However, it is in responding to questions that students sometimes work out what they think. Pausing at the end of an initial exchange prompts students to refine their first thoughts, and encourages them to self-correct, review their reasoning, and bounce ideas off their classmates.

Perhaps even more importantly, using pause time changes how you frame the role of questioning in your classroom.

You learn to listen interpretively

As a teacher, it is easy to rush to judge a student's answer: Is it correct? What have they left out? This evaluative response is reductive, narrowing your role in questioning to acknowledging when your students give the answer you hoped for, or "rescuing" them when they don't. Using pause time helps you avoid this impulse. Instead, it reminds you to listen interpretively (Davis, 1997). That is, to listen so you can ascertain how they came to their answer, and how you might modify your instruction to maximize their learning. This is particularly useful for partially correct answers or answers lacking detail and evidence, but crucial when a student has a misconception.

Using more pause time helps you to focus on the thinking behind your students' responses. However, it is not enough to just avoid the situation "where students report fixed answers to a teacher who then evaluates their responses as either right or wrong" (Reznitskya, 2012, p. 448). You also need to make space for students to offer those responses in the first place. As Pekrul and Levin (2007) succinctly put it, what student "voice requires is a listener" (p. 723).

You encourage student voice

As we examined in the last chapter, teachers tend to dominate class discussions. As a result, classes can become more like lectures, with questioning a prompt for students to "recall what someone else thought, not to articulate, examine, elaborate, or revise what they themselves thought" (Nystrand et al., 1997, p. 4).

You can't just tell your students to be active learners—you have to give them the time and space to do that active learning. Using pause time is an ongoing cue that our energies must be concentrated not on what we teach but on what students are learning. One of the teachers I coached summarized this really well: "Pausing after a student answers is a constant reminder that what matters is not how much of the curriculum I covered but how much of it my kids took in."

What does this mean in practice?

It means you need to spend time really working at not interrupting. Human conversation is shaped by unspoken turn-taking protocols and even a break of a couple of hundredths of a second is enough for you to feel like you should interject (Stivers et al., 2009). Don't. Students need a clear signal that they can discuss their thinking at length and without interruption. Most of the teachers I coach find that once they start extending their pause time they are able to elicit more frequent and deeper responses from their classes relatively quickly. However, getting started on including more extended pause times in your teaching is not always easy.

Of all the habits in this book, using extended pause time is one of the simplest changes to make in terms of technique. However, it is one of the hardest to put into practice. After all, using pause time sometimes seems counterintuitive: It can feel odd not to give your students instant feedback when they respond to you. Similarly, your students can feel a little lost without immediate affirmation or help when responding to your questions. This is where elaboration cues come in.

Elaboration cues

If you find using pause time difficult to implement you might want to try adding an elaboration cue before you pause. An elaboration cue is a quick signal to students that they should extend their answer. Once your students are used to being prompted to offer more depth and detail to their answers in this way, you can try using just pause time to do this even more seamlessly.

Here are some practical examples of elaboration cues you might use in your classroom:

Placeholder statements

It can be hard to just pause after a student answers—especially if your students are used to receiving a quick evaluation of their answer. If students are used to their teacher telling them their answer is correct or incorrect immediately, it can be disconcerting if, instead, all they do is pause. A placeholder statement is a good way to address this potential problem. Rather than silently pausing after a student answers, you can try offering a brief, noncommittal response:

OK . . .
Mmmm . . .
Oh . . .
Go on . . .

These phrases are sometimes called "minimal encouragers" and the key here is delivering them in a way that does "not imply agreement or disagreement" (I. Smith, 2009, p. 51).

I find that one of the easiest ways to do this is by responding in a drawn-out way with a rising inflection:

I s-e-e?

Y-e-a-h?

This signals to your students that you are not evaluating their response but looking for elaboration.

Blank prompts

Signaling that you don't fully grasp a student's response is an effective way to get class members to expand on their thoughts. Adopting a quizzical expression or feigning confusion, for example, will often lead to the student responding to clarify their thoughts for you. Some teachers go a step further and offer students a deliberately incorrect summary of their response:

So the Russian Revolution wasn't at all shaped by World War One?

Students are usually quick to pick up on teacher error and this approach often elicits a detailed clarification or correction from them. Blank prompts are often associated with elementary school classrooms. However, in my experience, they are just as effective with older students. Indeed, many students in high school take real pleasure in pointing out how their teacher "got it wrong." This strategy is a good way to emphasize to your students that justifying their responses with detail and examples is important; it reminds them that it is not enough to know something—we want them to be able to communicate this understanding to others.

Physical cues

You can use movement and gesture to encourage students to elaborate too. Many teachers have specific signals that they use to do this: rolling your hand, for example, in a "give-me-more" gesture or slowly stretching your thumb and forefinger apart to indicate to a student to "stretch out" their response. Alternatively, you might use physical cues to "guide students to notice something they might have missed" (Fisher & Frey, 2014, p. 48). This might include pointing to a board note or wall chart, or offering the student a resource with which to scaffold their answer.

Typically, students already know what these signals mean (either because they are commonly known, or because you have told them what they mean in your classroom), but some of the most effective cueing works more subconsciously.

I often coach teachers to drop their gaze and nod slowly after a student answers—the key here is not resuming eye contact with the rest of the class—and this often elicits further explanation from the student. Similarly, moving slowly toward a student after they answer often cues them to add further detail to their response.

Reflective statements

You can also elicit extended responses by answering students with a reflective statement. This is a classic active-listening technique, where paraphrasing back to someone what they said prompts them to clarify or add to their thoughts. When I coach teachers on how to adopt this technique, I suggest that they have some question stems in mind to make it easier to think of these statements on the spot:

> *Your answer then is . . .*
> *So what you are arguing . . .*
> *Your view is . . .*
> *It sounds like you are saying . . .*
> *Am I hearing right that . . .*

Prompts for wrong answers

In my experience, teachers often find it harder to use pause time after an incorrect response. There are probably a couple of reasons why this is the case. In coaching conversations, they usually cite the impulse to "rescue" students by providing the right answer, or a reluctance to let a wrong answer stand uncorrected lest it confuse other students.

It is worth learning some prompts you can use when responding to incorrect answers. Fisher and Frey (2014) have identified four main types of these prompts:

Background knowledge prompts. These remind your students of key facts that they might not have taken into account in their answer, prompting them to revisit their thinking:

> *Remember that an adjective is a word that describes a noun. Look again: What word in that sentence is an adjective?*
>
> *Knowing that red, blue, and yellow are the primary colors, how does the painter use secondary colors in this portrait?*

Process prompts. These remind students to use a procedure or approach that they have been taught already, but that they might have overlooked when formulating their answer:

I'm thinking of how we use BODMAS math to identify the order with which we approach this task. Where should we begin?

First you rewrite the prompt in your own words and then offer your contention. Given that's the case, what might your essay intro sound like?

Reflective prompts. These focus on metacognition, encouraging students to reflect on the effectiveness of their own thinking:

Why does that response make sense to you?

Listen to the question again: Did you really answer it?

How did you work that out to be true?

Heuristic prompts. I have always called these rule-of-thumb prompts: informal problem-solving strategies that might not work for every learner but could be a useful approach for a particular student:

I remember how to spell "because" by saying "big elephants can't always use small exits." Would that work for you?

You could try proofing your piece by reading it backwards—it is a great way to pick up on words you've misspelled. What would happen if you used that strategy?

When I first began using these strategies for responding to incorrect answers, I actually had to refer to a worksheet with examples of the prompts. This helped me to keep the four different styles of prompt clear. However, using them quickly became second nature and an important part of my questioning technique, and I have seen this pattern repeated with teachers I coach. If you are interested in learning this strategy, anticipate that, at first, it might take a bit of work to differentiate which prompt is which, but show some persistence because it will quickly become a practice that is instinctive.

Whole-class elaboration cues

It is easy to be a little myopic when you are trying to encourage elaboration. There are so many different techniques you can use to get a more detailed response from a particular student that you can focus all your attention on that student, forgetting that sometimes the best way to draw out an elaboration is to do it collaboratively. If a student is finding it hard to explain their response in more detail or justify their reasoning, you might use other members of the class or their group to help them flesh out their answer.

This is not just the "next-best" strategy for eliciting elaboration, it is often the most effective way to get students to unpack their thinking. Classroom discussion has a powerful impact on student performance (Hattie & Zierer, 2018) and part of the reason that this is the case is because students are getting to test their thinking out loud, bounce their ideas off one another, and build on each other's knowledge. These kinds of group responses are particularly important during learning phases where "questions may involve different perspectives or competing opinions" (Marzano & Simms, 2012, p. 64) and elaboration is one these phases.

Here are some questioning techniques you can employ to foster this sort of collaborative elaboration:

Inverted questions: The core skill we want to develop here is for our students to be able to add to a classmate's answer and discuss it in greater detail and depth. One of my favorite ways to build up this skill is to use inverted questions. This is where you take a traditional question:

>**Teacher:** *Is 5/4 an improper fraction?*
>
>**Student:** *Yes.*

and invert it so that the answer is included in the question stem. You then ask them to explain why this answer is correct.

>**Teacher:** *5/4 is an improper fraction. Why is this the case?*
>
>**Student:** *Well, an improper fraction is where the numerator is greater than the denominator and the numerator is five so that's bigger.*

Inverted questions tend to be richer questions to answer because instead of "fishing" for the right answer, you present it to students and then give them the higher-order task of justifying how or why they are correct.

This is a great precursor for collaborative elaboration because you are presenting these questions in essentially the same form as you do when "bouncing" questions to other students. The only difference is that instead of building on a peer's answer, they are elaborating on the answer provided in your inverted question. Students are used to being asked questions by their teacher, so this is a good way to build their confidence with this style of response before you ask them the more socially complex task of commenting on each other's answers.

Bounced questions: Instead of immediately evaluating a student's response ("Yes, that's right" or "Not quite, but good effort"), you can refer their response to another student to elaborate or comment on.

This is sometimes known as an IRF (Initiate, Response, Follow-Up) questioning pattern:

Initiate: *Why shouldn't athletes use performance-enhancing drugs?*

Response: *I think using performance-enhancing drugs is wrong not just because of cheating but because they are unsafe.*

Follow-Up: *Thanks, Manny. How might performance-enhancing drugs be unsafe? Santiago?*

Second Response: *Using steroids without checking with a doctor can give you a heart attack or stroke or you can end up in fights because of 'roid rage.*

I often use this term when I am coaching because it helps teachers distinguish bounced questions from the more common IRE (Initiate, Respond, Evaluate) questioning pattern, a pattern of questioning that tends to lead to less detailed discussion:

Initiate: *Why shouldn't athletes use performance-enhancing drugs?*

Response: *I think using performance-enhancing drugs is wrong not just because of cheating but because they are unsafe.*

Evaluate: *That's right, Manny, well done.*

I recently worked with a teacher who was struggling to get her students to elaborate in class discussion. When I suggested that she might try a different pattern of questioning she was adamant that this wouldn't be effective: "I have already tried mixing up the type of question I ask—low-order questions, high-order questions—nothing seems to work with these guys." A video analysis of a class discussion she led revealed that while she did vary the type of questions she asked, the *pattern* of questioning was always the same: After initiating a response from one of her students she would then discuss the answer, reviewing its accuracy.

Teachers can "crowd out" students by constantly mediating class discussion in this way (Burns & Myhill, 2004), and the teacher in question recognized this when she watched herself on video. She was able to address the issue very quickly by simply switching from an IRE question pattern to an IRF one and her students' contributions in class discussion began to steadily improve.

Wording bounced questions: If you are going to use bounced questions with your students, it is worth doing some thinking about how you might phrase these "follow-ups." Of course, you can just modify the elaboration cues discussed above, but there are some other techniques you might use too.

I like to ask students whether they agree or disagree with a classmate's answer and then get them to justify their thinking: "Mark, do you agree with Katzinka? Why is that?"

This lends itself to the kinds of "why" and "how" questions that generate more extended responses, as does asking students to build on the implications of a classmate's response:

> **Initiate:** *Group Two, what was the diet of sailors at the time? Mandy?*
>
> **Response:** *Dried peas, that hard tack biscuit stuff, salted meat, a little bit of cheese I think?*
>
> **Follow Up:** *That's a limited diet. What could be the effect of such a small number of ingredients in your diet—Holly?*

It is worth noting that Marzano and Simms (2012) have identified that the form of both of these types of question—questions that ask "why?" or "what are the effects?"—are particularly effective in the elaboration phase of learning. They have also suggested that "what if" questions where you ask students to project the implications of new learning into future situations are especially useful for generating elaboration:

> *What if there was a worldwide ban on coal-fired power plants?*

This reflects my own teaching experience. For example, when I taught history, questions that required my students "to predict what might happen (or might have happened) under certain conditions" (Marzano & Simms, 2012, p. 24) usually generated lots of extended responses from my students:

> *What if the gold rush had never occurred in California?*
>
> *What if the postwar immigration boom had never happened in Australia?*
>
> *What if the English Civil War had ended the monarchy forever in England?*

All three of these question types are great for eliciting elaboration from individual students but they are also great tools for asking students to extend and add detail to the thinking of their classmates. Keep them in mind when you are "bouncing questions" between students.

Eliciting responses

It is not just the phrasing of the question that you should be mindful of though—you can also help your students with how they word their answers to bounced questions. Building on another student's answer can be a challenging task. If some of your students lack the skill or confidence to take part in this kind of elaboration you can provide them with some sentence starters to help them:

I agree with _____'s response/prediction because . . .

I want to challenge _____'s answer because . . .

An example of what _____ is saying is . . .

Given what _____ told us, I predict that . . .

Sentence scaffolds like these reduce the language demands of the task—it is easier for a student to answer a follow-up question when you have provided them with the basic form the answer will take. Moreover, these sentences can help you shape the kind of answer you want, whether it is foregrounding what you want students to talk about ("The effect of this might be . . .") or just reminding them to be polite (in one school I worked at even the five- and six-year-olds contested each other's opinions by saying "I respectfully disagree with _____ because . . ."). You can hand out resource sheets with lists of these sentence scaffolds for students to paste in their workbooks, but most teachers find it just as easy to write them on the board before they conduct a class discussion.

An alternative strategy for creating an inclusive class discussion with follow-up questions is to get your students to use hand signals to indicate if they want to elaborate on an answer. I like to tell my students that if they want to add to an answer or challenge it, instead of putting up a hand to answer a question they should put up two fingers. This means when you are running a class discussion you can quickly delineate between those students who just want to answer a question or make a new point and those you can target to ask for elaborations.

Micro-data tools: Tracking pause time

Given the challenges involved with granting students more pause time, using a micro-data tool is a particularly useful mechanism for developing this skill. As the technique is similar to wait time, so are the tools we use to give us feedback on this technique.

Pause Time Dot Chart: The dot chart on page 88 is a modified version of the one we use for wait time: The person observing waits until a student gives an initial answer and then counts "one Mississippi." If they are interrupted in their count by the teacher talking, they put a tally mark in the left column. If they are not then they put a mark in the right column.

MICRO-DATA TOOL	
Pause Time Dot Chart	
Pause time < 1 second	Pause time > 1 second
TOTAL:	TOTAL:

A one-second pause is a low threshold but at first the gains here can be very small. Sometimes when I time pauses for teachers they actually get a negative number as they talk over the student's initial response—a phenomenon that is echoed in research (Wiliam, 2011). We therefore start with one second and build it up to "two Mississippi" and eventually three seconds. It is hard to record this data on your own because these initial gains can be so small, so if you don't have an observer it is best to record the exchanges between you and your students. Video is terrific because you can rewind and replay individual moments where you can clearly see how a subtle pause cued more elaboration or where you missed an opportunity to give a student more time to extend their answer.

Wait Time App: If you don't want to use the dot chart, there are some other ways to measure pause time data. I often adopt the wait time app (available at mcrel.org/tiltingyourteaching) for taking this data. The app was designed for wait time so one of the things it tallies is when your silence is less or greater than three seconds. This is too long a duration for adopting pause time, so I concentrate instead on the other figure it records: the average length of your silences. As the app gauges this down to hundredths of a second, you can measure subtle incremental improvements as your pause time improves.

Many teachers I have coached with this app have found that seeing these minor improvements reassured them that they were making progress as they worked toward the sometimes-challenging goal of making extended pause time an everyday habit. I have found asking teachers *how* these small gains were achieved is important for developing this habitual practice. Ask yourself after each session what helped you to pause a little longer and make sure you consciously repeat this in the next session. The key here is scaling your small successes, so the coaching question to consider is: If I did that lesson again what would I do the same?

Student Response Map: Alternatively, you can record which students offer a detailed answer with a class map. Just sketch a quick layout of the room, noting how the tables, desks, or workbenches are laid out and then mark on the map with an X where students responded to a question with more than a few words. With wait time we record this data with a class list, but for pause time it tends to work better this way because observers usually take this data, and this approach saves them from having to hunt for unfamiliar names on a class roll.

Bounced Question Map: Using a map as a micro-data tool also works well for whole-class elaboration: Ask your observer to record initial student responses to questions as a 1 on the map and then when you "bounce" their answer to another student for clarification or elaboration, record those responses as a 2. This gives you a quick-to-process visual of how you pattern your questioning when teasing out ideas in class discussion.

Many of the teachers I coach find that using a micro-data tool is the thing that tips their pause time from being an occasional strategy to a routine practice. It is well worth trialing some of these strategies to see what works for you.

Summing up

Patience is the key with all of these elaboration techniques.

Firstly, employing a strategy such as pause time takes patience: Holding back your responses till students have really finished their thought means taking your time, even when you feel like you need to rush to just get through the course. Keep in mind the idea of cognitive speed here. We often confuse the pace of the lesson with the speed with which students take up this information. Getting through the content means nothing if your students haven't learned it, so use your pauses to really gauge the extent of their understanding.

This can be particularly hard to do in situations where there is a lot of pressure on student grades. If you work in a school or school system where there is a lot of top-down pressure for teachers to "get good results" or if you are teaching a class with high-stakes testing looming, then it is understandable that you might feel pressure to rush. Remember though that even in situations where success is narrowly defined by summative assessment, what is being assessed is not the intended curriculum but the attained one. Pause time is not, in these circumstances, a delay to student learning but a way to ensure it. If you are feeling the pressure to rush your exchanges with your students, keep in mind that taking some time here will lead more quickly to deeper learning and better results.

However, it is not just employing pause time that requires patience, but also developing this technique. You have to give yourself time to cultivate the habit of pausing longer. Classroom discussions are not the same as the other conversations in which we take part. The subtle turn-taking conventions we pick up as young children and then use throughout our lives are not the same conventions we need to follow when we are facilitating whole-class or small-group discussions. If you are in the habit of responding to a pause of even 200 milliseconds in general conversation, it can take a while to learn to pause a little longer when you are teaching.

Similarly, it takes time to master the use of elaboration cues. I find that as long as teachers concentrate on learning one elaboration cue at a time, they pick up the individual techniques quite quickly. It can take a while though to learn to automatically select and implement the right strategy in the hectic back-and-forth of a class discussion, or even in a one-on-one discussion with a student. The key principle here is to stick with it. Through trial and error, you will get better at identifying which cue to use and when to use it. With practice, pause time will come to feel like an easy and natural part of interaction with your students.

Whenever I observe a teacher who is able to elicit lots of elaboration from their class, I ask them whether this is something that just occurs automatically in their teaching or if it's something that they have worked on. If I were to summarize their answers, it would be that it "happens automatically . . . now." This is the power of habit: It gives us a way to take something that is important but challenging to do and turn it into something we do without thinking. Pause time is an effective technique when consciously deployed with your students, but even more powerful when it becomes an instinctual part of your everyday practice.

Shift Six: Snapshot Feedback

Using fast, formative feedback from your students to assess the immediate impact of your teaching

Before I was a teacher, my only experience working with young people was as a junior basketball coach. When I started out teaching, I often compared the experience of coaching and teaching. One element that really struck me as different between these two contexts was how I approached feedback.

In basketball, when a player needed some coaching, I would usually be able to give the feedback immediately. For example, if a player tended to shoot free throws with their elbow crooked to one side, I would suggest straightening their arm during their shot and get them to immediately try again. In teaching, the situation was starkly different. If one of my students wrote a paragraph that wasn't closely aligned with their topic sentence, I would note this in my written feedback on their essay, return it to them the next class, and hope for them to apply this insight the next time they wrote an essay, which was usually days or even weeks later.

Sports coaches understand that feedback needs to be immediate, and immediately acted on, for the athlete to make the most of it. Obviously, giving written feedback differs from teaching physical skills in some important ways, but the basic point here still stands. As busy teachers, it is easy to find ourselves offering students feedback long after it would be most useful for them to hear it.

Our challenge is to find ways to give feedback that are analogous to basketball coaching: quick advice that can be given often (and easily) and that a student can put into action quickly. In my written work I often describe this feedback as "fast, formative and frequent" (Pearsall, 2012). In my experience, the Simple Shift strategy for developing this culture of feedback is being able to elicit snapshot feedback.

Snapshot feedback strategies are those techniques that you employ to get "instant" feedback about your class's performance. Typically, they are used in the middle of your lesson to get an idea of your students' current understanding, and how confident they are in applying that knowledge.

Schools use lots of different terms around the idea of feedback, so it is worth clarifying my language here: Many schools use *formative* feedback as a catchall term to describe these snapshot assessment techniques. However, specific feedback techniques are not inherently formative (or summative) as these terms don't describe the *type* of feedback you are using but *when* you are using it. Formative feedback is that which occurs *during* learning—when students can still act on this advice to modify their current performance—while summative feedback is given at the end of the learning sequence to describe their final result.

Snapshot feedback techniques, then, are used in the formative phase of the lesson, but what defines them is that they can be used and the feedback evaluated *quickly*. Ideally, snapshot feedback strategies allow you to check student progress without having to then mark the work or provide detailed written feedback—though there is also a place for exercises that require you to do some brief correction as long as it doesn't take too long to complete.

This emphasis on speed has two clear advantages:

Fast feedback is timely. As we have already discussed, the idea is that students get feedback that allows them to adjust what they are doing while learning is happening. Real-time feedback means you are receiving advice and correction at the precise moment when you can put this feedback into action. That young people prefer this kind of feedback should be obvious: Study computer games built for this audience and you will see how players receive feedback on their performance every few seconds, and this is no accident—game design depends on engaging their young audience. Just consider your own experience as a learner. Do you prefer to hear what you can do better in your teaching in the form of ongoing feedback, or would you like to hear it as a final judgment in an end-of-year review? Snapshot feedback gives kids advice when they are able to do something about it.

Fast feedback makes for better habits. It is easier to build a culture of fast, formative feedback in your classroom one small step at a time. Simple Shifts are the thin edge of a much larger wedge of strategies and habits. Instead of having to radically change everything about the way you approach feedback in the classroom, it is much simpler and quicker to trial some two-minute strategies and see if they work. As we discussed in the first chapter, James Clear (2018) calls these small changes of behavior "atomic habits" because they are small but a source of immense power. Clear would probably characterize snapshot feedback even more specifically as a "gateway habit": a small action that helps initiate larger routines. Rather than promising yourself you'll "read before bed every night," just try "reading a page" (p. 162). In my coaching experience, snapshot exercises are the teaching equivalents of these two-minute habits. They are small actions that can be the gateway to transforming the feedback culture of your classroom.

Feedback culture

What is so transformative about this type of feedback? It helps us remember that when we check for student understanding, we are actually not just assessing our students' progress but our own. After all, feedback is by definition a two-way process, or it isn't really feedback.

The idea that assessment is something that is solely focused on students is probably a view that formed when we were students ourselves. It is easy to imagine why as kids we thought that assessment was just something *done to us:* Assessment is the project you left till the last minute in elementary school or the pop quiz that was sprung on you in high school. "Feedback" then became your teacher's judgment of how you performed at these assessments.

This view of assessment and feedback can linger into adulthood, even amongst experienced educators. John Hattie, a renowned expert in assessment and feedback, acknowledges as much in his seminal work *Visible Learning* (2009): "The mistake I was making was seeing feedback as something teachers provided to students . . ." (p. 173). Instead, we need to view feedback as a way to assess the impact of our teaching: "It was only when I discovered that feedback was most powerful when it is from student to teacher that I started to understand it better" (p. 173).

Feedback is an opportunity to assess our students' depth of understanding contrasted against their past knowledge. It is a chance to evaluate what kind of errors they are making or misconceptions they have. It is a mechanism to gauge their level of engagement. In other words, feedback is a chance to assess whether our teaching is working. The snapshots we are taking are not just of our students' learning—they are of our own performance.

Snapshot strategies

Of course, what counts is what we actually do with these snapshots. If we find out that something isn't working and don't seek to change it, then snapshot feedback isn't very useful at all. ("In teaching, you don't have time to complain about something that *should* work," a mentor used to tell me. "Just focus on: *Did* it?") In terms of establishing this routine, though, the best starting point is trialing ways to solicit this feedback. Here are some practical examples of snapshot feedback that are both effective and easy to implement:

Private replay signals

You establish with students a prearranged signal they can send you if they want you to "replay" what you just covered. One colleague of mine, for example, asks his students to place a hand on their upper arm, while I get my kids to place a hand on their heart as a replay signal (though any unobtrusive gesture will do). When you see this signal, you recap the last thing you were talking about with the class. This might involve repeating an instruction or quickly clarifying an explanation. Usually this subtle rephrasing is not one that other students even notice. For instance, I often see teachers do this by finding a synonym for an unfamiliar word or redefining the key terms in an instruction:

> *We are exploring how juxtaposition is used in Les Murray's poetry.*
>
> **(Student Replay Signal)**
>
> *We are going to look into how Murray often put two images close together in his poems to create a contrast between them.*

In the flow of a lesson, this subtle addition takes a little extra time, but it might make a substantial difference to a student who is confused by what they are being asked to do. Similarly, just repeating what you said but at a slower pace can be helpful. Many students with slow processing speeds struggle to keep up because of the pace of instruction (Braaten & Willoughby, 2014, p. 4) and replaying what you said at a more measured pace is a quick and effective way to keep your lesson accessible.

When I first introduced replay signals in my own class, both of these strategies worked exceedingly well with my students. Perhaps too well: It was sobering to think that just by using more accessible language or speaking more slowly, I was able to clarify a lot of misunderstandings very quickly. How many students in my past lessons were confused because I wasn't conscious of these simple aspects of my teaching? This was powerful feedback.

Replay signals are easy to use, but there are some tips to keep in my mind when you are setting them up as a class routine:

Framing replay signals: We call them private replay signals but we introduce them to the whole class. The private part is that anyone can use the agreed-upon signal without the rest of the class having to know. You might be concerned that, despite the private nature of this exchange, your students will be reluctant to use this signal. It works best if you frame the replay signal as being about you rather than them:

> *I sometimes explain things badly or rush my instructions, so if I am not making sense to you, just let me know by using the replay signal. That way I'll know to say it again more clearly.*

My experience is that students are surprisingly enthusiastic about telling me how well I am teaching. If any of your students are still reluctant to employ a replay signal, you might want to establish an individual signal that only they use. Tapping a single finger on their cheek, placing a hand on their elbow, or putting a pen on the left corner of their desk are all successful examples that I have used with reluctant students without anyone else in the room even noticing.

Knowledge and procedure prompts: If you want to refine the wording of your replayed instruction, you can look to the prompts used in Shift Four: Wait Time. Fisher and Frey (2014) draw a distinction between "background knowledge prompts" and "process or procedural prompts" (pp. 48–49). This can be a useful way to think about how you rephrase your instruction: Does the student need me to be more explicit about the knowledge referred to in my instruction? Or do I need to clarify the procedure that I am referring to?

For example, look at this exchange transcribed from a video in a physical education class:

> *OK guys, we are going to line up at the door of the gym and practice receiving a pass and then having a shot on goal. Please be conscious of the offside rule.*

In the video, a student uses a replay signal at this point and the teacher reiterates that they will "line up at the door." The student looks even more confused. Given that the teacher was standing at the doorway and that students were already forming a line, it is more likely that the student needed the offside rule re-explained to them.

Being conscious of the background knowledge in the instruction might have led the teacher to a clearer reiteration:

> *So you're going to receive the ball—remember you can't be nearer to the goal than the ball or the second-last opponent, or you're offside—and then have a shot. Then return to the back of the line by the door.*

Alternatively, sometimes it is the process knowledge in your instruction that the student needs clarified. Here is an example where a teacher picked up on this:

> *Finish your first TEEL paragraph analysis (topic sentence, explanation, evidence, link) for* Edward Scissorhands *and then start the "T" for the scene where Edward cuts Peggy's hair.*
>
> **(Student Replay Signal)**
>
> *After we write our linking sentence, we start the next paragraph with the Topic Sentence again. What is your topic sentence for the haircut scene paragraph?*

The class had completed watching the memorable haircutting scene just the day before, so the teacher was quick to realize that it wasn't the text knowledge that was the issue but the TEEL structure that was confusing the student. Drawing a distinction between these two types of prompts makes it easier to formulate and target your "replayed" instruction.

Missing signals: When I coach teachers to use the replay signal, the most common concern they have is that they might miss their students' signals. And yes, you *will* inevitably miss some replay signals, but even if you miss some, you are getting 100 percent more than if you don't have a replay signal at all.

Public display signals

I visit many schools that have well-established public signals that students can use to indicate if they need help: a name plate that can be angled up, a paper cup that can be inverted. Hand signals are also quite common. One school I work at asks the students to signal with a thumb if they understand and a little finger if they need assistance.

However, probably the most effective version of this type of signal I see is using a two-sided marker:

Signal	I understand . . .	I need help . . .
Traffic light Colored disc with green on one side and amber on the other.	Green side of disc	Amber side of disc
Faces cards Circular card with caricatures (usually drawn by the students) of different expressions on either side.	Smiley face	Concerned face
Punctuation triangles Three-sided card with one side the base and the others an exclamation mark and a question mark.	Exclamation mark	Question mark
W/N card Laminated paper sheet about twice the size of a playing card with a capital N on one side and W on the other.	Working independently	Need help

This approach is popular and works well. As with replay signals, I find public displays work even better if you explicitly make the signal about the teacher. The W/N card, for instance, can be recast as *W* for "Well Explained" and *N* as "Need to Explain Better." Or the punctuation triangle can be explained to your students as advice to you: *!* represents "Keep teaching me this way" and *?* is, "Is this the only way you could teach me?" Reframing public display signals makes students less hesitant to indicate when they are struggling, and is a useful reminder that the snapshot feedback we are looking for is really about the *impact* of our teaching.

Extent signals

If you are assessing the impact of your teaching, it is important that you are not just asking "Is it working or not?" but "How *well* is it working?" (Pearsall, 2018). Learning is uneven, and introducing a skill or knowledge doesn't mean that students automatically realize what they are meant to understand, let alone that they can immediately master that skill or content knowledge. It is in the subtle increments of student growth where we must base the evaluation of our own teaching, and for this reason we need snapshot feedback that is focused on the *extent* of our students' learning.

The following snapshot feedback techniques assess the extent of your class's knowledge:

Thumbs Up, Thumbs Down: When I first started teaching I thought that this was a simple binary option: Holding a thumb up means "I understand," holding it down means "I don't get it." However, anyone who has used this in class knows that very quickly students turn this into an extent signal as they tilt their thumbs to a multitude of positions across the 180 degrees from totally upright to completely down. This wide spectrum of answers is particularly acute if you ask students to do Thumbs Up, Thumbs Down with two hands.

When I pause a video of this exercise in my workshops, teachers are often bemused at both the breadth of possible answers and the odd precision with which students indicate their answer when they use both thumbs—like they are setting the two dials on a 21-speed bike to get just the right gear. What is telling is that when I ask workshop audiences about individual student signals ("What does one thumb at 2 o'clock and the other at 9 o'clock mean?") there is usually quick consensus about what is the degree of the student's understanding. Thumbs Up, Thumbs Down gives you a quick, intuitive sense of the extent of your class's understanding, and the impact of your teaching.

Range: This technique is very similar to Thumbs Up, Thumbs Down, and I tend to introduce it in schools where Thumbs Up, Thumbs Down is associated with younger students.

It is very simple:

1. Ask students to hold their hands about a foot apart. Explain that this span indicates all of what they are expected to learn, which can be knowledge or a particular skill.

2. Now ask them to indicate how much of that knowledge or skill have they learned. About a foot apart means just starting out, six inches apart means halfway there, and fingers close together means they are nearly there. As with thumbs up and down, students tend to be quite precise about where on this range they are positioned.

3. This gives you a quick survey on how well your lesson is working so far. When I use this in my classes, I focus on mastery, either by asking students to indicate "how far to go before you could teach this to another student?" or "how much more do I have to teach you before you could pass this on to a new student?"

Traffic Lights: This snapshot feedback tool is traditionally used to assess how well students have understood your instruction. You explain the focus of the lesson and then get them to indicate their preparedness on a three-point scale:

- Green: *You explained it well—I'm ready to proceed.*
- Amber: *You explained it fairly well, but I just need some clarification before I proceed.*
- Red: *You didn't explain it well enough yet for me to proceed.*

Of course, you could use this three-point scale for any number of quick checks for understanding:

Rate how ready you are to teach this skill to someone else. Give me a quick traffic light rating—how engaging was this class? Green is: You are ready for the exam. Amber: You have one or two areas to revise. Red: You have a lot more studying to do before you feel confident.

Whichever approach you take, traffic lights are an easy-to-use, intuitive way to get students to move away from a binary understanding of learning ("I can do it/I can't do it") toward focusing more on the *extent* of their knowledge or skill.

Fist-to-Five: Probably my favorite way to take a snapshot of my impact is to use Fist-to-Five. With Fist-to-Five, you ask students to rank their level of understanding on a six-point scale using the fingers of one hand, from holding up a fist at the bottom of the scale through to displaying five fingers at the top. In this way, you can quickly ask students to map their understanding on a continuum from the early stages of encountering a specific skill or piece of knowledge right through to reaching a state of independent mastery.

Asking the class to give you a Fist-to-Five ranking of their progress is a simple and effective way to assess how your lesson is going, but there are a few tips to be mindful of to make the most of this technique:

Make it safe. There is always social risk involved in ranking activities—heightened here because the gap between someone who is giving themselves, say, a "one" and another student who gives themselves a "five" could be seen as so wide. Make sure then that your students don't feel threatened by having to display their ranking in front of the whole class. Some teachers (especially in elementary and primary schools) do this by asking kids to do Fist-to-Five with their eyes closed or close against their chests. However, I think it is better to reframe how you ask the question: When you introduce Fist-to-Five make all the rankings about your own performance; then once students feel more comfortable with this technique, move to a blend of ranking you and their own performance.

Be specific. The more precise you are about what each level of Fist-to-Five represents, the better your snapshot data will be. If you have time, outline to students exactly what each "finger" of the ranking represents. But remember, don't be too wordy—your students have to be able to quickly do a self-assessment:

> Hold up a fist to show you weren't here the last time we used gouache . . . three fingers if you know what both "staining" and "dry brushing" mean . . .

Anticipate talking. Students often give themselves a Fist-to-Five ranking and then start chatting to their neighbor about why they ranked themselves the way they did. (This happens so often that I have a colleague who calls this technique Fist-to-Five and Mutter.) Sometimes teachers block this discussion, but I think it is worth using some wait time here to actually encourage this discussion. Listen carefully to what the students are saying—very often they are reflecting on how well their approach is working and what they need to do better. This is feedback at the level of self-regulation, which is a very sophisticated level of feedback and something to be encouraged (Hattie & Zierer, 2018).

Appreciate precision. Even with six possible levels of response you will still have students who come up with their own intermediate rankings. For example, I was once modeling this exercise for an elementary school teacher and one of her students offered up a puzzling combination of extended and slightly crooked fingers. Confused, I asked him what this meant, and he responded: "That's a three point seven five." ("I'm just impressed," his teacher dryly added afterwards, "that he used decimals.") Think about what this actually means: I had offered him a six-point scale and instead he mapped it on a 24-point scale. Ranking himself a "three" or a "four" wasn't accurate enough for his self-assessment. Appreciate when your students slice their rankings even finer than the options you offered them—all those half-bent fingers show you that Fist-to-Five is really making students think about the extent of their (and your) performance.

Digital feedback systems

Technology has offered teachers a whole new set of ways to gather snapshot data. Each school I work in seems to have a new combination of device and software for collating data. At the moment, tablet computers, smartphones, and laptops with access to a school-based learning management system are popular, as are specific software suites such as Google Classroom, Kahootz, and Plickers. However, innovation in this field is exponential and any specific suggestions about what works well will quickly become dated. For our purposes, it is better to identify the strengths of the best digital feedback systems so you can recognize what to look for when working out what to use in your classroom.

Speed: The best feedback systems are fast and frictionless. You can ask students a question about your teaching or their learning and they respond immediately. This allows you to set up a short feedback loop to check your students' progress not just once at the end of the lesson but in real time as you teach. Slow login or sign-up times and labyrinthine options are real stumbling blocks in the middle of a lesson, so I try to dodge these inflection points by looking for easy-to-access hardware and software with few features that do one or two things well.

Accessibility: Many snapshot feedback activities require students to be able to complete certain movements or tasks. Think about how many of the signaling activities mentioned above could be problematic if you weren't mindful of differentiating for students who don't have full control of their limbs. Digital feedback systems tend to be less physically demanding than some of these activities. They also often have a lower barrier of entry for students with language or literacy needs, with built-in accessibility functions for students with disabilities. Finally, they provide students with an element of privacy for communicating with the teacher, which is particularly useful for those who might feel self-conscious about struggling with their work.

Anonymity: Digital feedback systems provide students with a genuinely anonymous way of commenting on your teaching. I often meet teachers who switch to an electronic feedback system and are surprised by the increased volume (and sometimes vehemence) of the feedback they then receive. Of course, we have to be clear to students that, as always, we won't tolerate abuse. Not having to put their names to their feedback, though, gives students license to really tell you what they think—and you to honestly assess your impact.

Data storage: Perhaps the biggest advantage of these systems is not only that you can quickly check for understanding, but that this information is collated and saved for you. In the busy environment of a classroom, it is hard to solicit, analyze, *and record* data. Digital feedback systems give you an easy way to sort and store this data for further analysis. That this can be done at scale—say with a large, open-learning class group of 60 students—with no extra effort really underlines the advantages of the best of these digital feedback systems.

Extended snapshot feedback

What is the difference between snapshot feedback and all the other feedback you seek out in the course of the lesson? As we have seen, essentially the difference is how quickly you can request and review this feedback. If it takes less than a couple of minutes to assess how your lesson is going, then it is a useful snapshot strategy. If it takes more than that, then probably snapshot feedback is just another thing you are being asked to include in your lesson . . . and it is probably far less likely that it will become an everyday teaching habit.

The challenge for accomplished teachers who have mastered many of the simple strategies above is how to solicit even more sophisticated data from students without breaking this time barrier. There are a couple of strategies that are worth trialing here:

Mini whiteboards

A mini whiteboard is a letter-sized wipe-clean surface that students can use to write on. I like using mini whiteboards in class because they are a means for students to not just *tell* you what they understand, but also to quickly *show* you. How do you use them? Simply ask your class to answer a key question about the topic you have just explored or summarize what they have just learned on their whiteboards. They then all hold up their mini whiteboards and you can scan for errors and mistakes and note particularly strong responses.

I have written extensively elsewhere about the advantages of using these boards (Pearsall, 2018), but one of the key advantages in this context is that they help you quickly target the effect of your teaching for students of different abilities. Using mini whiteboards is a particularly good way to differentiate your teaching, because it is easy to spot misconceptions (something that other snapshot techniques miss because it is by definition impossible for students to self-report a misconception) and to identify students who might need to be further extended. Moreover, kids don't view their whiteboard answers as their final answer, so they are less hesitant about showing you their work and you get a clear picture of their "first draft" thinking.

Hinge questions

A hinge question is a multiple-choice question that you use to ascertain how well your students understand what you have just taught them. Do they understand what I was just teaching? Can I move to the next part of the learning? Or do I need to revisit what I just taught? If they are making mistakes what types of misconceptions do they have?

Unlike other techniques in this chapter, it is time-consuming to prepare a good hinge question. Finding a good question doesn't take long, but creating revealing distractors (the wrong answers in a multiple choice test) can be difficult.

Look at the example below:

What Is The Central Idea Of The Poem?

A: Plath, who was ambivalent about having children and prone to depression, describes her daughter Frieda's birth in 1961.

B: The speaker is ambivalent about motherhood, but surprised by her growing love for her newborn daughter by the end of the poem.

C: Plath is depressed by the birth of her child and ambivalent about motherhood, though she does experience some growing love for her baby at the end of the poem.

D: This poem explores complex associations we attach to motherhood, asking what it means when we say motherhood is a "natural" experience.

While none of the answers necessarily do justice to Plath's poem, the teacher has written the distractors (responses A–C) to help identify students who are falling into common misconceptions about poetry analysis:

- Answer A targets students who confuse biographical study with analyzing a poem.
- Answer B targets students who summarize the poem rather than analyze it.
- Answer C targets students who confuse the poet with the speaker.

While these questions are time-consuming to create, the trade-off is that they are a very efficient use of time in a class. In this example, the teacher can use a short two-minute exercise to establish which students misunderstand the fundamental nature of the task long before any of them even put pen to paper. (Or the teacher has had to correct a pile of essays full of misconceptions about what the task is.) And once a good hinge question has been created, it can be used with the same curriculum again, which ultimately saves even more time.

Hinge questions are emblematic of the best elements of snapshot feedback: They are a fast but rigorous way to assess student progress, and one of my favorite ways to quickly check the impact of my teaching.

Tracking snapshot feedback

In schools where I run small-group video coaching, teachers are usually quick to adopt snapshot feedback as part of their planning, but getting these teachers to use a micro-data tool pushes this a step further, as it increases the amount of *impromptu* snapshot feedback they seek out. Using a data tool to record Opportunities to Respond (OTRs) is a simple but effective way to make using snapshot feedback an everyday teaching habit.

Opportunities to Respond Tally: The easiest way to measure your use of snapshot feedback is to use an Opportunities to Respond Tally micro-data tool. I first encountered OTRs as a measurement used in the coaching of classroom management (Sprick et al., 2006), as increasing student response opportunities often reduces the number of off-task behaviors you encounter in the classroom (Moore et al., 2010). I've found that tracking OTRs is a useful way to develop the habit of using snapshot feedback.

The key is making sure your observer knows precisely what to look for when recording OTRs. There are lots of different ways to elicit feedback from students, so discuss the range of techniques you might use with the person who is going to watch your lesson. (Note that to emphasize the importance of this step, it is something you are asked to include on the OTR Tally.) This is a good way to cue your observer what to be on the lookout for and to remind you of your options. Once you and your observer are clear about what constitutes an opportunity to respond, recording this data is a straightforward process.

Whenever you give a student an opportunity to give you feedback—whether it's a quick nonverbal signal such as a Fist-to-Five or a more extended opportunity such as a hinge question—you record this as a mark in a tally sheet like the one below.

If you want to take this a step further, you can draw a circle around the dot or dash if this was a whole-class feedback activity to distinguish between these opportunities and those that target individual students. Alternatively, you can put a 1 for an individual piece of feedback and the number of students in your class (26) for whole-class feedback. Both of these techniques help you quickly assess whether you are getting the balance of whole-class and individual feedback you were aiming for.

MICRO-DATA TOOL

Opportunities to Respond Tally

Opportunities to Respond (OTRs)	Total OTRs:
Examples of the types of OTRs that the observer should look for in your lesson:	

Snapshot Feedback

Opportunities to Respond App: You can also use an app to record OTRs (available at mcrel.org/tiltingyourteaching). While this tool doesn't distinguish between whole-class and individual feedback, it does record *when* you asked for each piece of feedback, so it gives you a sense of the frequency and the spacing of OTRs you offer students. This is helpful data for planning and reviewing your use of snapshot feedback—particularly for working out when is the most effective point during the lesson to seek out this feedback.

Opportunities to Respond are a simple data point to record, so you may just want to take this data yourself. In my experience, making the tally chart small enough to fit in one hand makes it easier to quickly note whenever you check for student understanding. Once you have the data, ask yourself: How many students in this class could I name as having met the learning goal of the lesson? (One teacher I know uses a roll to do this because "otherwise I just think of the *usual suspects*.") If there are lots of students you are unsure of, try and identify at what other point in the lesson you could have asked for more feedback. How many more OTRs would be required to meet this goal? Try and reach this mark the next time you are teaching a similar lesson. Even without the support of a peer coach or professional learning team, I have seen this approach lead to substantial changes in the way individual teachers seek out feedback.

Whether you use an app or paper tally chart, a peer partner or take the data yourself, OTRs are a highly effective way to remind ourselves of a central point of this chapter—that it is not what we *teach* students that matters but what they *learn*.

Summing up

I am sometimes asked by school leaders to assign some professional reading for their staff to help their teachers understand the theory behind formative feedback. There are lots of excellent pieces you can read on the value of continuously assessing the impact of your teaching; Chapter 1 of Hattie & Zierer's *10 Mindframes for Visible Learning* (2018) is a good recent example. However, as I mentioned at the beginning of this chapter, I think that sometimes it is better to trial snapshot feedback techniques in your classroom than read the theory of why they work.

This is because the Simple Shift here is focusing on the students' voices. Regularly seeking out what your students are thinking about the lesson can be a powerful driver for refining what you do. There is a big difference between suspecting that a couple of students might not have fully grasped the point of a lesson, and hearing directly from several students that they don't understand at all and really need your help. Your students provide a countervailing force to all the back-of-the-head pressures—the ticking clock, the pages of content-heavy syllabus not yet covered—that loom over us as teachers and prompt the feeling that we have to "get through" the course. After all, the best test of effective teaching is the same one we use for taking students on a field trip or a class excursion: Success is not just getting across the finish line but being able to bring everyone with us. Building in time to ask your students what they think provides constant reminders that despite other pressures, this is our real goal.

Don't try to employ every snapshot feedback technique at once. Target a technique you think might work and spend a few weeks trialing it intermittently. Discover what works in your subject or at your students' age level or with your class. Let your students get used to the logistics of writing exit tickets or using Fist-to-Five, and then see if their responses start to influence what you do. This is a "bottom up" rather than "top down" way of fostering change, and I think understanding this point makes it a lot easier to implement. Rather than snapshot feedback being yet another task for teachers, remembering that it is a way to understand your students' needs—and make both learning and teaching easier—is a compelling motivation for establishing it as a routine.

Trialing this handful of snapshot feedback strategies will help you start to establish formative feedback routines. Indeed, some schools I have worked with found that just getting teachers to test a few of these techniques led to more lasting change of teacher habits than all the work they had previously put into embedding formative feedback into their instructional model. Sometimes, it seems, it is easier to alter your thinking by changing your actions than it is to change your actions by altering your thinking.

Shift Seven: Reflection Time

Giving students an opportunity to quickly *demonstrate* that they have taken on your advice

I once coached a teacher who spent an enormous amount of time marking up student work. She would annotate every aspect of her students' essays with thoughtful and detailed comments which were carefully color-coded so that she could link them to a series of summary statements and a long list of "feed-forward" advice for students to enact in their next essays. She was inordinately proud of her efforts.

I was asked to coach her, though, because all this effort was immensely stressful and when she was particularly busy (report-writing time being a case in point), this stress affected her deeply. My plan was to reduce the scope of her marking so that her stress levels were lower.

The problem was that she was deeply reluctant to change her practice: "I shouldn't be doing less—everyone else should be doing more!" As a solution, I videotaped her students receiving their feedback and showed her how few of them read her comments—instead they just looked at the mark and then put the marked-up work back in their folders. She was adamant that this was because we had given them a shorter than usual amount of time to explore her comments. We repeated the exercise the next time she gave students their work back, doubling the time they had to review the comments. This time a majority of students just looked at their grade and then used the extra time to find out what their friends got. The teacher was sobered by this proof that the impact of her marking was in no way commensurate with the effort she was putting in.

As a teacher, it is easy to concentrate on the quality of the advice you give, but the real test of feedback is what students do with it. Good feedback is productive: "The most important feature of effective feedback . . . is that it leads to useful action on the part of the student" (Wiliam & Leahy, 2015, p. 109). Teachers are constantly providing students with direction, advice, and feedback. The only really effective way to measure the quality of this feedback is to ask ourselves: To what extent did my students actually act on it? Did they respond to my advice? Did my students take up my suggestions? Did they make changes to their work based on my comments?

There is a wide body of research and literature on feedback that you can use to hone your advice to students (Fisher & Frey, 2014; Hattie & Clarke, 2018; Pearsall, 2018), but the Simple Shift I want to focus on here is giving students the time and framework for responding to this advice. This seems obvious, but it is striking how often in the hectic environment of the classroom that this doesn't happen. As we have already seen in Shifts Four and Five, teacher talk takes up a disproportionate amount of class time and opportunities for student voice are often limited (Littleton et al., 2005; Nystrand et al., 1997). Routinely giving students enough time to respond to your advice is a keystone habit that will maximize the effect of your feedback.

The fact that this is so often overlooked is hardly surprising. Faced with the pressure of an entire course to get through and the demands of supporting students of very different abilities and needs, it is easy to see why a teacher who is rushed for time might skip over this step to squeeze in more instruction or give more expert advice.

Sometimes, though, "we need to stop talking and listen for our impact" (Hattie & Zierer, 2018, p. 3). We have already explored how questioning and snapshot feedback can be used to do this, but making space for students to show us that they have explicitly understood our instruction is an important strategy too. There are two main areas where this is particularly useful: when you want to establish the learning purpose of a lesson (or group of lessons) and when you are providing students with written feedback on their work.

What links these areas is that they are both areas of practice where teachers tend to play a predominant role, but actually work better when students are more actively involved. You can spend a lot of time formulating effective learning intentions and success criteria, but what really matters is that your students actually use them as a reference point as they work toward their goals. Similarly, you can spend huge amounts of time marking up and correcting your students' work, but the key issue is whether your students actively use it to revise and refine their work. Having ways to elicit more student voice in these two areas of practice can substantially improve your students' learning while reducing your workload.

Let's look at how we might go about doing this for each of these aspects of teaching and learning.

Learning Purpose

The idea behind focusing on learning purpose is simple: We want students to understand what they are learning and how they can tell when they have reached this goal (Wiggins & McTighe, 2005). How can students do this if they don't know what success looks like? This clarification is crucial because students often confuse the activity they are doing with the learning that underpins it: As Bryan Goodwin and Elizabeth Ross Hubbell (2013) observe, "It's easy for students to lose sight of the why that underlies *what* they're doing in the classroom" (p. 28).

It is for this reason that providing your students with a clear description of what they are learning in the form of a learning intention has become increasingly popular in schools, as has providing a success criterion against which they can measure their progress. However, as mentioned above, the challenge is getting students to take on this advice. Learning intentions and success criteria can easily become something you carefully plan and present to the class, but aren't really used by the students. I have seen many lessons where they become "wallpaper objectives": something the teacher displays on the whiteboard and their students dutifully copy down but are not referred to again (Wiliam, 2011, p. 56).

This is where providing students with reflection time comes in: By asking them to quickly demonstrate that they understand the learning purpose of the lesson they are much more likely to internalize these goals. We want them to use learning intentions and success criteria as a compass point: a reference by which to steer their efforts in your classroom. Here are some techniques to embed reflection time in your classroom.

Scrutinizing

There are a number of quick ways to get your students to "unpack" learning intentions and success criteria:

Highlighting: This is one of my favorite ways to get students to explore a learning intention. It is also probably one of the easiest.

Traditionally, highlighting has been the preserve of the teacher:

> **Learning Intention:** *We are learning how to revise our topic sentences to remove ambiguity.*
>
> **Teacher:** *OK, let's look at the learning intention: The key word here is "revise." Please highlight that for me.*

However, when you ask *students* to choose what to highlight, they have to really scrutinize the learning intention properly. One of the most effective ways to do this is to ask your students to highlight what is unclear in the learning intention:

> *OK, let's look at the learning intention. Can you please underline any word that you think someone else might find unclear?*

In the learning intention above, it might be that a struggling student is comfortable with the word "revise," but unsure of what "ambiguity" means. Framing the question around what "someone else" might struggle with gives the students a safe way to flag this or anything else they might not understand about the learning goal. It also gives you feedback about how clearly you are communicating your learning intention.

Evaluating: If you want your students to scrutinize success criteria with a similar intensity, you could try getting them to rank or rate these criteria. For example, you might ask students to give each of the success criteria a mark out of 10 as to how hard they will be to achieve. Or you might ask students to rank the individual success criteria, from easiest to achieve to the most personally challenging. Again, this will not only cue students to study the success criteria more closely but also give you feedback about which criteria your students are least confident about achieving.

Each of these exercises takes little class time, but will give your students the chance to demonstrate whether you have made the learning direction clear.

Rewriting

Another way to do this is to require students to redraft the language of a learning goal—ask your students to rewrite a learning intention in their own words. I always do this in pairs or groups of three:

> **Learning Intention:** *We are learning the process for maintaining an orderly and risk-free work environment while using the lathe.*
>
> **Rewritten:** *We are learning the steps to keep our workstations clean and stay safe when using the lathe.*

While this usually only takes a few minutes, the task encourages students to really examine what the intention is asking of them. They can check with each other for clarification about specific words, see if others share their presumptions and, together, try and find language that reflects their mutual understanding.

It is important to note that your students don't have to rewrite the learning intention well for this activity to be successful. If a group of students struggles to rewrite a learning intention, then that is useful feedback that some of them might not understand the learning goal. Moreover, this activity makes the goal not just relevant ("you should know it") but resonant ("you want to know it"). In my experience, students who have had trouble completing the rewriting task are then much more likely to listen when you "unpack" it because they find out what their answer could have been.

In a relatively short time, students get comfortable with rewriting and this makes it a helpful precursor activity for other, more challenging activities for demonstrating their understanding.

Cocreation

Obviously, one of the ways to ensure students have a clear learning goal is to get them to design their own, but this is not always possible. The mandated nature of the curriculum and the time-intensive nature of creating your own goal can make it difficult to set this task for students. Asking students to *cocreate* learning intention statements with you, though, is a good alternative. It is a practical way to get the benefits of this type of approach without the logistical challenges, or having to accommodate the strictures of the formal curriculum.

Here are two of my favorites:

Prediction: There are many versions of this type of activity. You can present students with an activity and ask them to predict what the learning intention of the activity might be, or you can provide students with a learning intention and get them to guess what the success criteria might entail. I know a teacher who presents students with a model answer and then asks them to guess what the learning intention and success criteria will be based on this exemplar. He calls the activity Learning Purpose Lotto. Whatever version of prediction you use, these activities get students to closely examine your learning advice and think about the design and nature of learning intentions and success criteria, and what goes into making and using them.

Adding criteria: You present your class with a learning intention and part of the success criteria, and ask them to create the rest. A good starting point is giving students the learning intention and three examples of success criteria, and asking them to provide the fourth. Students tend to master this activity quite quickly, and you may find that you can graduate faster than you had expected to asking them to add two or three of the criteria—or even just creating their own success criteria entirely. When I first started doing this activity, I would often have a firm expectation of what I wanted for the fourth criterion. I was struck by how often students would come up with two or three different and better examples than the one I had in mind.

"Adding criteria" can be done verbally with the class—ideal for very young kids or those who struggle with their literacy—or quickly on paper, and is a great way to demystify how to use success criteria.

Personalization

This is a hybrid of a revision and a cocreation task where you ask your students to revise learning goals to give them a personal slant. The key to doing this effectively is providing them with some scaffolding: You need to "model the process for your students and provide them with sentence stems" (Goodwin & Hubbell, 2013, p. 27). At many schools where I coach staff, teachers will get students to write "I can" statements to describe their goals:

I can . . . work independently.

I can . . . confidently multiply three-digit numbers.

Or they focus on helping students personalize their goals by drawing on their curiosity:

> *I want to know . . . what would happen if you were in a car struck by lightning.*
>
> *I want to know . . . why a woman, even in that time, would think Mr. Collins was a good match.*

Sometimes you can help students formulate goals by giving them question stems that bounce off gaps in their knowledge:

> *I want to know more about . . . photosynthesis.*
>
> *I know . . . what happened at the storming of the Bastille but I want to know . . . why it happened.*

These are useful ways to get students thinking about what they are learning, but when I coach teachers, I prefer to get them to concentrate first on how students will know they have reached their goal.

Look at the example below:

Success Criteria

Your paragraph should:
- contain a topic sentence
- be written in the active voice starting with the subject
- cite textual evidence

I will be successful if I have:
- introduced my main idea in a strong opening sentence
- started sentences with the characters' names first
- used quotes from the book to back up what I'm saying

Using the "I will be successful if . . ." stem ("I have achieved my goal when . . ." also works), this student has been able to revise the criteria so that he knows precisely what success in this task looks like for him. His teacher also gets a sense of what he might not understand. (If the student above had written "starting sentences with the characters' names or the author's" in the second criterion, then the teacher could be more confident that they fully understand what the subject is and what constitutes an active voice.) Asking your students to personalize success criteria is a great way for them to demonstrate how well they understand your advice.

Unpacking models

Learning Purpose. Success Criteria. Learning Intention. These can seem like abstract phrases to your students—teacher terms not really connected to the work in front of them. Some schools address this by changing the terminology. I know a number of elementary schools that use the more concrete terms WALT (we are learning today) and WILF (what I'm looking for) to replace learning intentions and success criteria. However, I have always found that the easiest way to make the connection between learning purpose and student work is to use model answers. By asking students to draw learning advice from student exemplars and other model responses, you make it clear that these terms are not part of an empty routine but a description of concrete things they can do to make their work better. Here are two classroom-tested examples of how you might do this:

Ranked models: Present your students with several examples of student work and then ask them to put the models in rank order from the strongest to the weakest. Ranked modeling is a productive way to use modeling in class, because in offering students multiple work samples, it avoids the biggest trap of giving students a model answer: that they will simply copy it. Instead, when asked to rank responses, they look for shared elements and patterns across responses. Students can then use the common features of the strongest responses to build success criteria and "reverse engineer" a successful answer of their own. I like that this produces both better and more diverse responses from my students.

I also like how quickly you can complete this task. This exercise uses relative comparison—where you make a "like-for-like" comparison between similar work products, without reference to external criteria. This seems to quickly give students an intuitive sense of what a good answer looks like. A ranked modeling activity is an ideal way to check that students understand the goal you have given them before they start their work.

Inverted models: In this activity, you present students with a weak model containing all the things you don't want them to do in their own work. They then analyze this piece to make a "what to avoid" list to use when completing the task themselves. In my experience, students tend to be deficit markers: They focus on the flaws in model answers. Therefore, it is not surprising that students often treat this exercise with real glee, pointing out all the errors in the inverted model. They show even more joy if you ask them to create a flawed example themselves. You can then have them annotate this example, pointing out its weaknesses.

Both versions of this activity work as effective ways to quickly show students what they need to avoid, helping them produce a high-quality answer. However, a word of warning is required here. This is not something you would try the first time you introduced a particular task—that would only confuse students (especially those who struggle). Nor is it a set-and-forget independent work task: this exercise requires close supervision. You don't want students to confuse the instruction to make a bad work sample with making an inappropriate one, or students focusing their criticism of the work on its author ("they must be so stupid") instead of the errors they make in analysis. And you would never assign this task for homework where, without context, parents might misinterpret the instruction to their children to produce the worst answer they can. However, with careful monitoring these kinds of risks can be avoided.

If we want to make the most of the learning purpose advice we offer students, then we have to build time into the curriculum for them to show us that they have genuinely grappled with this advice. These exercises are good ways to start developing this habit.

Feedback advice

Marking makes up such a substantial part of an average teacher's workload, but there isn't actually a lot of rigorous research you can look at to determine the best ways to mark-up student work. A recent survey of the research on written marking found that despite "enormous amount of effort invested in marking books" there is "a very small number of robust studies" that look at this everyday aspect of teaching (Elliott et al., 2016, p. 4).

One tentative finding that is useful here is that students need time in class to reflect on written advice: "There is a strong case for providing dedicated time to consider and respond to marking in class" (Elliott et al., 2016, p. 16). This makes sense: Why correct something if students aren't going to read and react to your advice? Unfortunately, this happens all the time in schools. When I help teachers with their marking technique, I often get an opportunity to flick through student workbooks. It is striking how often I will find an insightful and carefully composed comment and then see that same comment repeated with subtle variations (and an increasing vehemence) throughout the rest of the workbook.

Creating a regular reflection time when students can demonstrate whether or not they have understood and acted on your advice is the best way to avoid this trap. There are many different strategies you can use to cue students to respond to your specific written comments, and developing a toolbox of techniques will enable you and your students to get the most out of your written feedback.

Two-step annotation

One of the simplest ways to ensure students respond to your feedback is to make sure that they have an explicit role proscribed to them for even the simplest of annotations.

Minimal marking: This technique, which is also known as "error flagging," is easy to use. When you find a surface error in a student's work, put a check mark in the margin on the line where the error has been made and leave your student to find where the mistake has occurred within that sentence and correct it. Designed many years ago as a shortcut to reduce teacher workload (Haswell, 1983, 2006), minimal marking is an important technique because it signals to students that even when you are picking up low-level mistakes, their job is not just to read your annotations but to answer them.

You need to be mindful when using this technique that it is aimed at surface errors—spelling mistakes, minor factual inaccuracies, and simple calculation errors. These are not mistakes of understanding, but errors resulting from inattention, lack of effort, or carelessness that students can readily self-correct. You cannot use this technique where the error reflects a deeper misconception because the student will not know how to fix it, no matter how often or clearly it is flagged.

You can modify this technique to suit your students or subject. For more guidance, you can circle the word that is misspelled, or give a check mark to each letter of the word that is correct, but still expect students to self-correct their error.

If you don't primarily mark written work (if teaching math or accounting, for example), then you might use "error counting" instead. This is where, rather than mark each individual calculation as right or wrong, you group them and provide an overall mark (9 out of 10, 4 out of 8) and the student needs to identify which of the answers is wrong.

Double ticking: When you find a particularly successful element of your student's work, you indicate this with a double check mark (tick), or a short superlative of some kind ("excellent," "first rate!"). Your students are then expected to explain why this part of their work was so successful.

In Australia, the majority of teachers I work with will "double tick" something that is done exceptionally well in a piece of work, while overseas teachers are more likely to give a one- or two-word compliment. What is less common everywhere is having an established convention that students need to respond to this annotation by explaining why precisely the teacher has highlighted this example. I think this is missing an opportunity: We don't just double tick to affirm students, we do it to encourage them to repeat this approach in future work, to "scale" their success.

Asking students to respond to your comments on the work itself (or in a notebook or reflection journal) does two important things. Firstly, it clarifies to the student why they have received this positive feedback. When asked, students often can't explain why their teacher double ticked their work, or can only explain it in the most general terms. This exercise quickly addresses this issue. Secondly, by asking students to describe and reflect on their success, it makes them more conscious of what they did well and, in my experience, more likely to use this approach in future work.

This is an excellent stepping-stone activity for helping students build up the skills to take part in other, more time-intensive forms of correction, such as dialogic and triple-impact marking (see Elliott et al., 2016). However, it is also a terrific stand-alone exercise for giving you a chance to see if they understand your positive comments about their work.

Summaries and commentaries

Teachers often closely annotate student work and then summarize their comments as key feedback, but there is no reason that you should always do both of these things. With some training, your students should be able to share this responsibility with you. The key to making this work is the training. We want to carefully scaffold the process so that students gradually build up their ability to be more actively involved in marking their own work.

Summaries: The first step in this process is asking students to rewrite your summary comment. This helps them be more conscious of the form of these comments, and is in itself an effective way for them to demonstrate their understanding of your feedback.

The second step is to teach them how to look for patterns in your annotations of their work. You want your students to be able to recognize the main ideas in your feedback, and see that your annotations are not just a list of corrected mistakes, but an attempt to show you the types of mistakes they have made.

A good way to teach this is to use an "error cluster" exercise where you present students with an exemplar response and a table listing common types of errors. (This approach works equally well if you give them a list of common strengths.) Then as a class—and later in pairs with a different model answer—they identify which comment refers to which type of error. For much younger students, you can do a version of this activity with error cards, a series of laminated sentences that either don't have a capital at the start or a full stop at the end. In teams, they can sort them into separate piles representing each type of common error, giving them an introduction to error patterns and types.

Once students have some experience clustering individual teacher comments, you can ask them to write a summary comment addressing the two or three most common pieces of advice. When they are confident doing this, you can ask them to write out these summary comments with their own work whenever you return work to them.

Annotations: After students have mastered writing summary comments based on your corrections, you can teach them to annotate their own work based on your summary comments. One way to do this is to model the kinds of corrections you want them to make on a section of their work, then ask them to apply these insights to the rest of their response. If I am correcting a student's visual analysis of a painting, for example, I might correct the first body paragraph of their piece and then ask them to demonstrate what they have learned by doing the same for the remaining paragraphs.

Another way to scaffold this is by writing your summary comments in the form of questions. This gives students a more concrete sense of what they need to do as they correct their own work. Compare these versions of the same advice:

> *You need to use adjectives in your sentences to create a more atmospheric setting for your story.*
>
> *Could you add adjectives to any of the sentences where you are describing the setting to make your story more atmospheric?*

The advice in the second summary comment is clearer and more specific and therefore easier for students to act on—especially those just learning to self-mark their own work.

Framing your comment as a question doesn't only help with the clarity and specificity of your comments, but also with finding the right tone. Susan Brookhart (2008) suggests that to be "heard," the tone of your feedback should be respectful, frame the student as an active learner, and cue curiosity and reflection. When you frame your advice as a question, you can achieve this tone: Simply by adjusting the way you phrase your comments, you are asking rather than telling, positioning the student as someone who can answer, and encouraging the student to wonder about an answer.

Teaching your students to be able to annotate their work based on your general comments is an ambitious goal, but it is one that is worth the effort. I don't know a better way for students to demonstrate their understanding of your feedback than being able to put it into action by applying it to their own work in a detailed way.

Immediate review exercises

In each of the strategies we have explored so far we have been asking our students to respond to what could be characterized as "response and review" marking. Shirley Clarke (2014) defines this type of marking as "the practice of marking children's work away from them, highlighting the best bits and suggesting improvements" (p. 139). In her work, Clarke contrasts this type of marking with the advantages of within-lesson feedback, which she says is often more collaborative and immediate, arguing that teachers should blend these approaches.

We have already discussed how we can use questioning and snapshot responses to create this fast feedback loop. I should also make clear that, to some extent, asking young people to reply to response and review marking is a form of within-lesson feedback itself. However, it is worth asking: In what other ways can we ask our students to respond in real time to demonstrate they understand our feedback?

Feedback stamps: Teachers give students lots of oral feedback in the course of a lesson. In video coaching sessions, educators are often struck by how much one-on-one advice they give out just as they circulate around the room. Just as with written feedback, we need to ensure students understand and act on the verbal advice they are given.

A good way to check if this advice is reaching students is getting them to summarize it back to you. I encourage the teachers I coach to use a stamp worded "My summary of the teacher's verbal feedback:" to do this. (If their students only work in soft copy, then I get them to write the same thing on their student's keyboard in a dedicated font or color.) You can then stamp your students' work and ask them to write a précis of your advice, which can be reviewed when you next move past their desk or as an exit pass as they leave the classroom.

Many teachers get students to do their summaries verbally, but I prefer this approach because it makes the history of your verbal feedback visible both to you and your students, as well as to their parents or guardians. However, if you are concerned about the language demands of the task—say for very young students or those who might struggle in the class's target language—you might try using a visual stamp, with symbols that represent the common types of advice given. Students then need to match the symbol with the advice, and show they have done this by checking a box.

Student exemplar: This activity is something you can use after students have been working independently (on their own or in teams), and you want to quickly check on their progress. Pause the class and display an interesting work-in-progress example of what the class is doing. I usually take a photo of a student exemplar and project it, but you might just ask the student to read or display their draft work or get them to copy it out on the whiteboard. As a class, you then discuss both the strengths of the response and its areas for potential improvement. Once this discussion has ended, your students modify their work based on what they have learned unpacking the exemplar.

Cooperative feedback: This is the collaborative version of the previous task. This time students complete it in pairs, looking at their own and their partner's work. Some of the teachers I have coached have been reluctant to use peer feedback exercises like this one. They worry about unevenly matched pairs and students receiving shallow or insensitive feedback. These are legitimate concerns, as working in pairs can be logistically difficult and receiving feedback can be a fraught experience. Indeed, we know that even good feedback can be rejected for all sorts of reasons (Stone & Heen, 2014).

However, there is a way to work around a lot of these concerns. The key is that rather than swapping work, students focus on one piece of work at a time and review it together. This single adjustment has a profound effect on how your students experience peer reflection. Instead of reviewing and then writing comments on their partner's work, they discuss the strengths and potential areas for improvement of one piece of work as a pair. The student whose work it is (and only that student) makes any changes they think are helpful based on this feedback. They then repeat this process with the other piece of work.

This is a versatile activity that works with all kinds of written pieces and work examples. Whether you do it as a collaborative task or a whole-class discussion, it is an engaging way to create some time in your class for students to demonstrate their take-up of your advice.

Micro-data tools—tracking reflection time

Reflection time is a routine designed to help you shift the locus of learning from you to your students. There are several data points you can use to help you build reflection time into your lessons and to assess whether it is working to encourage student voice.

OTRs Tool: One obvious starting point is to look at opportunities to respond. Whether you use the paper tally sheet (Shift Six: Snapshot Feedback) or the app version at mcrel.org/tiltingyourteaching, OTRs are a simple metric to record that can give you a sense of whether you are giving students enough reflection opportunities. My work in video observation suggests teachers tend to offer students chances to respond during class discussion, but not as frequently when explaining the learning intention or returning marked-up work. If you provide reflection time during these phases of the lesson, the number of OTRs will go up substantially—making OTRs a clear metric to watch if you want to establish reflection time as a routine practice.

Learning Intention Data Tool: Alternatively, you can explore the depth and frequency with which you employ learning outcomes such as learning intentions and success criteria. The most common flaw with directions is that they become something you pay cursory attention to at the start of the lesson: You put them on the board, students copy them down, and "the lesson proceeds without further reference to the learning outcomes" (Wiliam & Leahy, 2015, p. 28). The Learning Intention Data Tool chart on the next page addresses this issue.

It not only gives you an opportunity to tally how many times you and your students refer to learning outcomes but at what point in the lesson this happens. The tool breaks the lesson into three phases: the introductory phase when you are first unpacking learning intentions and success criteria with students; the development phase when students are engaged with collaborative and independent learning and checking with these learning outcomes to assess their progress; and the review phase where the class reviews their progress against these goals. I have found this micro-data tool to be an invaluable feedback device for helping teachers encourage their students to really engage with the learning purpose. It is particularly useful for reminding you to offer students proper opportunities to unpack the learning purpose in greater detail at the start of the lesson and then encouraging them to refer to this learning purpose as a compass point throughout the rest of the lesson.

MICRO-DATA TOOL

Learning Intention Data Tool	
Phases	**Specific references to learning intentions (May be to whole class or to individual students)**
Introductory Phase _____ minutes *Introducing learning intentions*	
Development Phase _____ minutes *Formative review of learning intentions*	
Review Phase _____ minutes *Reflecting on extent of student achievement*	

The app version of this tool (available at mcrel.org/tiltingyourteaching) is laid out in exactly the same way.

While originally designed for exploring learning intentions, I have found it works equally well for getting data on how you help students unpack and refer to success criteria in the course of a lesson. The micro-data it records is presented in a color-coded pie graph that is a striking way to visualize when and to what degree you and your students refer to the learning purpose throughout the lesson. This data can be sobering: One teacher reviewing the graph with me suggested that the development phase tab might not be working until she realized with a rueful grin that actually she had only referred to the success criteria at the start and end of the lesson. But it is very useful feedback as you try to maximize the effect of exploring learning purposes with your students.

Whether using the app or the paper version of this tool, the coaching questions I ask are almost always the same: Could you have more frequent mention of the learning intention/success criteria in the body of the lesson? Did students have enough time at the end of the lesson to assess whether they met these goals? When reflecting on this data you might want to start with these questions.

Focused Task Time Tool: Another way to measure the impact of using reflection time is to examine the ratio of teacher to student voice in your classroom. There are a number of tools designed to assess how much of the lesson involves the teacher giving instruction versus the students making sense of the instruction through reflection and collaboration. For example, you might use Jim Knight's (2018) popular "teacher talk vs. student talk" chart in which you time the respective amount of time each of you speaks in a lesson (pp. 176–177). However, I prefer to use a Focused Task Time tool because you can more easily use it yourself in class (timing who is speaking can be difficult when you are one of the speakers) and it provides a space for registering when teacher and students are in conversation with each other. Moreover, it is a more visually arresting tool, which I think can be important for at-a-glance prompting of behavioral change.

How does the Focused Task Time tool work? You divide the lesson into one- or two-minute blocks, then shade in any block where, for the majority of that period, students are not just listening to instruction but actively working—either independently or with their peers (see an example of the Focused Task Time tool on the next page). If your instruction takes up the majority of that time, leave the square blank. If instruction and active student work are split fairly evenly—say in a class discussion—then shade half the block.

The resultant patchwork is compelling visual feedback of the split between instruction and student work time in your class.

MICRO-DATA TOOL

Focused Task Time Tool (60-minute class in 2-minute blocks)				
0:00–0:02	0:02–0:04	0:04–0:06	0:06–0:08	0:08–0:10
0:10–0:12	0:12–0:14	0:14–0:16	0:16–0:18	0:18–0:20
0:20–0:22	0:22–0:24	0:24–0:26	0:26–0:28	0:28–0:30
0:30–0:32	0:32–0:34	0:34–0:36	0:36–0:38	0:38–0:40
0:40–0:42	0:42–0:44	0:44–0:46	0:46–0:48	0:48–0:50
0:50–0:52	0:52–0:54	0:54–0:56	0:56–0:58	0:58–0:00

The app version of this tool, again available at mcrel.org/tiltingyourteaching, records similar information to the paper Focused Task Time tool, but instead of presenting this as a series of blocks of time, it uses a timer to prompt you to make this assessment at intervals throughout the lesson. It then presents this data in a color-coded graph. I recently used this tool to observe a lesson in which a teacher was handing back written comments on student essays.

Reviewing the graph, the teacher was struck almost immediately by how little time his students spent reflecting on his comments versus how long he spent giving students an overview of their import. This is a good example of the way you can use the app to quickly make you more aware of how you divide up class time between instruction and student reflection.

Building more reflection time into your lessons is often seen as something you do through lesson planning. These tools remind us that it is also a matter of honing our instruction and being more alert to opportunities when we might give students a chance to reflect on our advice as we deliver the lesson.

Summing up

Allocating dedicated reflection time into lessons can feel like a zero-sum game: *If I give students time to demonstrate the learning goals or show me they have understood my written feedback, that gives me less time to actually teach.* Intellectually, we can understand that this is confusing the *pace* of how we get through the content with the *cognitive speed* with which students master it. Emotionally, though, it is hard not to feel the need to *teach* as well as we can—to devote our energy to explaining, refining, and reiterating the material for our students—rather than spending time finding out what our students have learned.

If it feels counterintuitive to use these reflection time strategies, go about it at a deliberate pace. Start small. Pick one or two strategies and test them in your class. Did they work within your context? Was the time they took to implement worth the effect they had on your students? If you start adopting this approach more broadly it will be because you can see the benefits of it for your students. Similarly, if you wish to convince others of the validity of this approach (much of the design of courses and allocation of lesson time is actually decided at the team and school level) it is better to be able to show people the result of reflection time on your students, rather than expect them to change their beliefs because of your advocacy alone.

Make sure you don't just create an empty space in the lesson for students and expect them to produce feedback for you without any guidance. Provide your students with the scaffolding to guide their reflection. Focus on a narrow, clearly defined set of skills and keep the activities brief. When you are introducing these activities, be clear with your class about what precisely you are hoping they will get out of it. Provide lots of support as they are working.

At the end of the activity, where possible, check in with your students to see if the exercise was helpful: Did coming up with a title for each dot point in the criteria sheet help them understand what they had to do in the task? Did writing a summary of your commentary make it clearer how they could improve their essay? Each opportunity for reflection time then becomes a chance for students to get better at voicing their reflection, so they can gradually take more ownership of this process.

This is crucial because learning is a partnership and we need to constantly encourage students to take an active role in their own learning. With all the things teachers have to do in a lesson, we can forget that students have a prominent role to play in every aspect of learning—and they can likewise assume that we are *solely responsible* for their progress.

We have already seen how we can shift this dynamic through the use of questioning strategies such as wait and pause time, as well as snapshot feedback techniques. Reflection time augments these strategies by focusing on two areas—learning objectives and written feedback—where student voices are traditionally muted. This makes it a particularly important strategy for building an active learning culture in your classroom.

After all, our success as teachers is not defined by what we deliver to students, but what they gain from this instruction. Reflection time reminds us all that the classroom is not just where students are taught but where they come to *learn*.

Conclusion: A New Way of Looking at Teaching

It is easy to see the success or failure of a lesson in moral terms: Are we good or bad at our job? Did we try hard enough? Spend enough time planning or reviewing student work? This isn't the most helpful way to view the craft of teaching. The morality in teaching is that *you chose to do it in the first place*. I rarely meet teachers who got into teaching because of the enormous sums of money they expected to earn, or the reverence they will receive in the community. (You're at a supermarket checkout, and the person ahead of you in line notices you: "Sorry, you're a teacher—I didn't realize. Step ahead of me in the line. Move aside, guys! That's a *teacher* coming through.") We go into teaching because we are interested in learning. We want to work with young people. We want to give something back to our community. These are vocational reasons—but how to get the most out of this vocational commitment is about technique.

One of the inspirations for this book was the video coaching work I have done with educators on the nuances of technique. Initially the appeal of video for me was that teachers could see their lessons from the outside, from the perspective of the students in the classroom. Looking at your teaching through the eyes of your students is a powerful source of insight, and for many educators it is a point of view that really changes their approach to teaching.

However, there is another benefit to video coaching that I didn't anticipate: You can rewind and rewatch specific classroom moments again and again. Video allows you to isolate the precise technique that changed a student's behavior or identify the exact exchange that ramped up their level of engagement. Often these small adjustments of routine or variation of technique are so subtle that, as an observer, you don't even notice them on the first viewing. Sometimes teachers themselves aren't even aware of these moments. Experienced teachers can be surprised when they see themselves employing strategies that they weren't aware they even used—because they have developed them to the point of unconscious routine. (*I did do that didn't I!*)

What strikes you most as you spend a lot of time viewing and reviewing these moments is how subtle the difference between good and great teaching can be. How adding an extra moment of pause time led to a student offering a more detailed and thoughtful response. How the deft use of a pivot phrase de-escalated a situation and nudged a student back to their studies. This is an exciting prospect: If you wish to get better at the demanding craft of teaching, sometimes the best use of your energies is to make some of these micro-adjustments of practice.

You can see the appeal of this idea in small-group video coaching sessions. Once a teacher has recognized which Simple Shift strategy they should have used in the lesson excerpt they recorded, they are usually quick to adopt it into their practice—and you will often see that change of practice demonstrated in their very next video. Moreover, there is a lot of cross-fertilization of ideas that goes on with teachers adopting techniques and insights from each other's videos. It seems that in the hectic world of teaching, small changes of practice are both easier to adopt and to spread.

I started to think of these strategies as somehow different, though, because not only did they help teachers change these small aspects of their practice but, over time, their mindset too. Throughout this book we have come back to this idea again and again—that new strategies can change your teaching, but over time they will change your thinking too.

Teachers who are trying out a Simple Shift are effectively running a series of small practical experiments. At first you are assessing whether the approach will work in a specific instance with a specific student. However, if these little trials are successful, you may start to think that this is the *type* of strategy that you will employ in other situations. In fact, eventually the presumptions that underpin this type of strategy can start to become your own: If using pause time in your class repeatedly leads to individual students offering more detailed responses, then eventually you may come to see elaboration not just as a matter of *ability* but one of *opportunity*.

This mindset shift is not just having a new view of how to generate elaboration, but a new sense of yourself: *I am the type of teacher who uses pause time to generate more detailed responses from my students.* Identity is a powerful motivator for behavior change (Cialdini, 2000). Many of the dramatic improvements I see in video coaching sessions can be attributed to the mindset shift associated with identity. Early on in the program as teachers trial techniques, the pace of behavioral change among the group is steady. But once teachers start to view specific approaches as being part of their identity, the adoption of new practice takes off exponentially as they bring *all* their teaching practice in line with their new view of how they do things. If you *are* a questioner who uses a lot of pause time, then adopting more reflective listening and elaboration techniques is just a natural extension of your identity.

This is the power of Simple Shifts. They are small changes of practice that are relatively easy and quick to adopt but because you are what you repeatedly do, they ultimately have the power to shape your identity as a teacher.

Of course, the biggest impact these Simple Shifts can have is not on you but on your students. I run video coaching at many schools, but while writing this book I have kept thinking about my experiences of two schools in particular. One is an elementary school in the southwest of Melbourne. The other is a large, outer-suburban K–12 campus. Both are relatively new schools, dealing with substantial social and economic disadvantage in the school communities but addressing these challenges with real energy and dedication. I have worked with both of these schools for a long period of time, so my video coaching program has given me a window into the growing skill and sophistication of the instructional practice at these institutions. More than that, though, I have seen students appear in snapshot moments across their school life. It is powerful to see a Grade 3 student who couldn't sit in his seat, politely and earnestly taking part in class discussion in Grade 6, or remember a shy Year 8 student who has become an articulate and able class leader in the final year of her studies.

Obviously, I can't claim that any one strategy I saw teachers use with these students caused these transformations . . . and yet it is the compounding effect of these strategies used repeatedly over years of schooling that helps foster these changes. In the midst of a busy classroom on a Thursday afternoon it is hard to see the impact of these subtle little interactions, but over the longer view their impact is profound.

This book is an attempt to offer teachers a handful of simple strategies that you can use to maximize this impact. I hope that it helps you in your everyday teaching—the heroic project of helping young people, one modest little gesture at a time.

References

Bennett, B., & Smilanich, P. (1994). *Classroom management: A thinking and caring approach.* Bookation Inc.

Black, P., & Wiliam, D. (2014). *Inside the black box: Raising standards through classroom assessment.* Learning Sciences International.

Braaten, E., & Willoughby, B. (2014). *Bright kids who can't keep up: Help your child overcome slow processing speed and succeed in a fast-paced world.* Guilford Press.

Brookhart, S. M. (2008). *How to give effective feedback to your students.* ASCD.

Burns, C., & Myhill, D. (2004). Interactive or inactive? A consideration of the nature of the interaction in whole-class teaching. *Cambridge Journal of Education, 34*(1), 35–49.

Campbell, M., Kenway, C., & Pearsall, G. (2017). *Toon Teach* [Animated series]. Teacher Training Australia.

Cazden, C. B. (2001). *Classroom discourse: The language of teaching and learning.* Heinemann.

Cialdini, R. B. (2000). *Influence: Science and practice* (4th ed.). Allyn and Bacon.

Clarke, S. (2014). *Outstanding formative assessment: Culture and practice.* Hodder Education.

Clear, J. (2018). *Atomic habits: An easy and proven way to build good habits and break bad ones.* Penguin Random House.

Davis, B. (1997). Listening for differences: An evolving conception of mathematics teaching. *Journal for Research in Mathematics Education, 28*(3), 355–376.

Dix, P. (2017). *When the adults change, everything changes: Seismic shifts in school behavior.* Independent Thinking Press.

Duhigg, C. (2014). *The power of habit: Why we do what we do in life and business.* Random House.

Elliott, V., Baird, J., Hopfenbeck, T. N., Ingram, J., Thompson, I., Usher, N., Zantout, M., Richardson, J., & Coleman, R. (2016, April). *A marked improvement? A review of the evidence on written marking.* Education Endowment Foundation, University of Oxford.

Fisher, D., & Frey, N. (2014). *Checking for understanding: Formative assessment techniques for your classroom* (2nd ed.). ASCD.

Gollwitzer, P. M. (1999). Implementation intentions: Strong effects of simple plans. *American Psychologist, 54*(7), 493–503.

Goodwin, B., & Hubbell, E. R. (2013). *The 12 touchstones of good teaching: A checklist for staying focused every day.* ASCD.

Guise, S. (2013). *Mini habits: Smaller habits, bigger results.* Selective Entertainment LLC.

Harkin, B., Webb, T. L., Chang, B. P. I., Prestwich, A., Conner, M., Kellar, I., Benn, Y., & Sheeran, P. (2016). Does monitoring goal progress promote goal attainment? A meta-analysis of the experimental evidence. *Psychological Bulletin, 142*(2), 198–229.

Haswell, R. H. (1983). Minimal marking. *College English, 45*(6), 600–604.

Haswell, R. H. (2006). The complexities of responding to student writing; or, looking for shortcuts via the road of excess. *Across the Disciplines.* http://wac.colostate.edu/atd/articles/haswell2006.cfm

Hattie, J. (2009). *Visible learning: A synthesis of over 800 meta-analyses relating to achievement.* Routledge.

Hattie, J. (2012). *Visible learning for teachers: Maximizing impact on learning.* Routledge.

Hattie, J., & Clarke, S. (2018). *Visible learning feedback.* Routledge.

Hattie, J., & Zierer, K. (2018). *10 mindframes for visible learning: Teaching for success.* Routledge.

Kahneman, D. (2011). *Thinking, fast and slow.* Farrar, Straus and Giroux.

Kegan, R., & Lahey, L. L. (2012). *How the way we talk can change the way we work: Seven languages for transformation.* [Ebook]. Jossey-Bass.

Knight, J. (2018). *The impact cycle: What instructional coaches should do to foster powerful improvements in teaching*. Corwin Press.

Lemov, D. (2010). *Teach like a champion: 49 techniques that put students on the path to college*. Jossey-Bass.

Lemov, D. (2015). *Teach like a champion 2.0: 62 techniques that put students on the path to college*. Jossey-Bass.

Lewis, R. (2012). *The developmental management approach to classroom behavior: Responding to individual needs*. ACER Press.

Littleton, K., Mercer, N., Dawes, L., Wegerif, R., Rowe, D., & Sams, C. (2005). Talking and thinking together at Key Stage 1. *Early years: An international journal of research and development, 25*(2), 167–182.

Mackay, J. (2006). *Coat of many pockets: Managing classroom interactions*. ACER Press.

Maroni, B., Pontecorvo, C., & Gnisci, A. (2008, March). Turn-taking in classroom interactions: Overlapping, interruptions and pauses in primary school. *European Journal of Psychology of Education, 23*(1), 59–76.

Marzano, R. J., Pickering, D. J., & Heflebower, T. (2010). *The highly engaged classroom*. Marzano Resources.

Marzano, R. J., & Simms, J. A. (2012). *Questioning sequences in the classroom*. Hawker Brownlow.

Marzano, R. J. (2017). *The new art and science of teaching*. Solution Tree.

Moore, T., Robertson, R., Maggin, D., Oliver, R., & Wehby, J. H. (2010). Using teacher praise and opportunities to respond to promote appropriate student behaviour. *Preventing school failure 54*(3), 172–178.

Nystrand, M., Gamoran, A., Kachur, R., & Prendergast, C. (1997). *Opening dialogue: Understanding the dynamics of language and learning in the English classroom*. Teachers College Press.

Olson, C. B. (2011). *The reading/writing connection: Strategies for teaching and learning in the secondary classroom* (3rd ed.). Pearson.

Partin, T. C. M., Robertson, R. E., Maggin, D. M., Oliver, R. M., & Wehby, J. H. (2010). Using teacher praise and opportunities to respond to promote appropriate student behavior. *Preventing School Failure: Alternative Education for Children and Youth, 54*(3), 172–178.

Pekrul S., & Levin B. (2007). Building student voice for school improvement. In D. Thiessen & A. Cook-Sather (Eds.), *International Handbook of Student Experience in Elementary and Secondary School* (pp. 711–726). Springer.

Pearsall, G. (2012). *Classroom dynamics: A teacher's handbook.* TLN Press.

Pearsall, G. (2018). *Fast and effective assessment: How to reduce your workload and improve student learning.* ASCD.

Pink, D. (2009). *Drive: The surprising truth about what motivates us.* Riverhead Books.

Pope, G. (2013). *Questioning technique pocketbook.* Teachers' Pocketbooks.

Reznitskaya, A. (2012). Dialogic teaching: Rethinking language use during literature discussions. *The Reading Teacher, 65*(7), 446–456.

Rogers, B. (2015). *Classroom behaviour: A practical guide to effective teaching, behaviour management and colleague support.* SAGE.

Rowe, M. B. (1972, April). *Wait-time and rewards as instructional variables: Their influence in language, logic and fate control* [Paper presentation]. Annual meeting of the National Association for Research on Science Teaching, Chicago, IL, United States.

Rumhor, F. (2013). Reflection and inquiry in stages of learning practice. *Teaching Artist Journal, 11*(4), 224–233.

Sheerhan, P. (2002). Intention—behavior relations: A conceptual and empirical review. *European Review of Social Psychology, 12*(1), 1–36.

Sherrington, T. (2013, January 6). Behaviour management: A Bill Rogers top ten. *Teacherhead.* https://teacherhead.com/2013/01/06/behaviour-management-a-bill-rogers-top-10/

Smith, I. (2009). *Assessment and learning pocketbook.* Teachers' Pocketbooks.

Smith, D., Fisher, D., & Frey, N. (2015). *Better than carrots or sticks: Restorative practices for positive classroom management.* ASCD.

Sprick, R., Knight, J., Reinke, W. M., & McKale, T. (2006). *Coaching Classroom Management.* Pacific Northwest Publishing.

Stahl, R. J. (1994). Using "think-time" and "wait-time" skillfully in the classroom. *ERIC Digest.* ERIC Clearinghouse for Social Studies/Social Science Education.

Stivers, T., Enfield, N. J., Brown, P., Englert, C., Hayashi, M., Heinemann, T., Hoymann, G., Rossano, F., de Ruiter, J. P., Yoon, K.-E., & Levinson, S. C. (2009). Universals and cultural variation in turn-taking in conversation. *Proceedings of the National Academy of Sciences June 2009, 106*(26), 10587–10592.

Stone, D., & Heen, S. (2014). *Thanks for the feedback: The science and art of receiving feedback well.* Penguin.

Tobin, K. (1987). The role of wait time in higher cognitive level learning. *Review of Education Research 57*(1), 69–95.

Walsh, J. A., & Sattes, E. D. (2016). *Quality Questioning: Research-based practice to engage every learner.* Sage Publications Inc.

Wiggins, G., & McTighe, J. (2005). *Understanding by Design* (2nd Expanded edition). ASCD.

Wiliam, D. (2011). *Embedded formative assessment.* Solution Tree.

Wiliam, D., & Leahy, S. (2015). *Embedding formative assessment: Practical techniques for K–12 classrooms.* Learning Sciences International.

Wiliam, D. (2016). *Leadership for teacher learning: Creating a culture where all teachers improve so that all students succeed.* Learning Sciences International.

About the Authors

Glen Pearsall was a teacher leader at Eltham School and board member of the Victorian Curriculum Assessment Authority in Australia. He was also a research fellow at the Centre for Youth Research, University of Melbourne. Glen is the author of the best-selling *And Gladly Teach* and *Classroom Dynamics*, and co-author of *Literature for Life* and *Work Right*. He works throughout the world as an educational consultant, specializing in instructional practice, teacher coaching, and workload reduction for teachers. He is a Cambridge Education associate and a master class presenter for the Australian professional development organization TTA, and has a long association with the Teacher Learning Network. Glen is also the founding presenter of the widely popular PD in the Pub series for graduate and pre-service teachers. His most recent projects include *Toon Teach*, an animated series on classroom management, and *Fast and Effective Assessment: How to Reduce Your Workload and Improve Student Learning*, which was published internationally by ASCD.

Natasha Harris is an editor and professional writer. She was the managing editor of *Traffic*, the University of Melbourne's journal for interdisciplinary studies, and has worked on such educational publications as *The Music Cubby* and *The Literature Toolbox*. Natasha has a long-term interest in behavior change and skill acquisition, and worked in communications at Research and Innovation, RMIT University. She is currently the production editor of *Australian Birdlife* magazine.

Reproducibles

MICRO-DATA TOOL

Affirmations vs. Commands Chart

Affirmations	Commands
Any time you acknowledge success or endorse behavior.	Any time you tell a student what to do, give instructions, or challenge off-task behaviors.
"Fast transition, guys. Excellent." *"Have a look at Li's answer here—this is how this question should be approached. . . ."* *"You asked three people before you asked me. Good initiative."* *"This group alerted others to the rallying call. Well done."*	*"Everyone get in pairs and then line up against the wall."* *"Everyone, please look this way."* *"Come here. You are not to speak to me like that again. Is that understood?"* *"Stop it, Michael. That is not appropriate."*

© McREL International. You may make copies of this page for personal classroom use only. To request permission for broader use of this reproducible, please contact McREL International at info@mcrel.org.

MICRO-DATA TOOL

Attention Cues Tally

Verbal interventions
Repeating your instruction, naming the student and directing them to comply, discussing the impact of the student with the student, etc.

Nonverbal interventions
Using hand signals, facial expressions, or your spacing in the room to cue the student to pay attention.

TOTAL:

TOTAL:

© McREL International. You may make copies of this page for personal classroom use only. To request permission for broader use of this reproducible, please contact McREL International at info@mcrel.org.

MICRO-DATA TOOL

Wait Time Dot Chart

Wait time < 3 seconds	Wait time > 3 seconds
TOTAL:	TOTAL:

MICRO-DATA TOOL

Pause Time Dot Chart

Pause time < 1 second	Pause time > 1 second
TOTAL:	TOTAL:

© McREL International. You may make copies of this page for personal classroom use only. To request permission for broader use of this reproducible, please contact McREL International at info@mcrel.org.

MICRO-DATA TOOL

Transitions Scaffold Checklist

Use a rallying call to demand *attention*.	State *when* students are going to move.	State *what* it is they are about to do.

© McREL International. You may make copies of this page for personal classroom use only. To request permission for broader use of this reproducible, please contact McREL International at info@mcrel.org.

MICRO-DATA TOOL

Transitions Scaffold Checklist (*continued*)

Explain *who* they will work with in the next activity.	Give the students the *move now* signal.	*Monitor* the transition using teacher proximity.	Give specific feedback about the transition.

© McREL International. You may make copies of this page for personal classroom use only. To request permission for broader use of this reproducible, please contact McREL International at info@mcrel.org.

MICRO-DATA TOOL

Opportunities to Respond Tally

Opportunities to Respond (OTRs)	Total OTRs:

Examples of the types of OTRs that the observer should look for in your lesson:

© McREL International. You may make copies of this page for personal classroom use only. To request permission for broader use of this reproducible, please contact McREL International at info@mcrel.org.

MICRO-DATA TOOL

Learning Intention Data Tool

Phases	Specific references to learning intentions (May be to whole class or to individual students)
Introductory Phase _____ minutes *Introducing learning intentions*	
Development Phase _____ minutes *Formative review of learning intentions*	
Review Phase _____ minutes *Reflecting on extent of student achievement*	

© McREL International. You may make copies of this page for personal classroom use only. To request permission for broader use of this reproducible, please contact McREL International at info@mcrel.org.

MICRO-DATA TOOL

Focused Task Time Tool
(60-minute class in 2-minute blocks)

0:00–0:02	0:02–0:04	0:04–0:06	0:06–0:08	0:08–0:10
0:10–0:12	0:12–0:14	0:14–0:16	0:16–0:18	0:18–0:20
0:20–0:22	0:22–0:24	0:24–0:26	0:26–0:28	0:28–0:30
0:30–0:32	0:32–0:34	0:34–0:36	0:36–0:38	0:38–0:40
0:40–0:42	0:42–0:44	0:44–0:46	0:46–0:48	0:48–0:50
0:50–0:52	0:52–0:54	0:54–0:56	0:56–0:58	0:58–0:00

© McREL International. You may make copies of this page for personal classroom use only. To request permission for broader use of this reproducible, please contact McREL International at info@mcrel.org.